THE MOUNTAIN BIKER'S GUIDE TO
THE LAKE DISTRICT

By the same authors:

THE MOUNTAIN BIKER'S GUIDE TO THE RIDGEWAY

Forthcoming titles in this series are likely to include:

The Yorkshire Dales and North Yorkshire Moors
The South Downs
Dartmoor and Exmoor
North Wales
The Brecon Beacons
The Peak District
Northumberland, the Borders and Southern Scotland
The Scottish Highlands

THE MOUNTAIN BIKER'S GUIDE TO

THE
LAKE DISTRICT

Andy Bull and Frank Barrett

STANLEY PAUL

LONDON   SYDNEY   AUCKLAND   JOHANNESBURG

Stanley Paul & Co. Ltd
An imprint of the Random Century Group

20 Vauxhall Bridge Road
London SW1V 2SA

Random Century Australia (Pty) Ltd
20 Alfred Street, Milsons Point, Sydney, NSW 2061

Random Century New Zealand Limited
191 Archers Road, PO Box 40–086, Auckland 10

Century Hutchinson South Africa (Pty) Ltd
PO Box 337, Bergvlei 2012, South Africa

First published 1991

Set in Plantin by 𝔽 Tek Art Ltd,
Addiscombe, Croydon, Surrey

Printed and bound in Great Britain by
Martins of Berwick

A CiP catalogue record for this title is available from the
British Library

ISBN 0 09 1746450

This book is dedicated with our grateful thanks to Andy Leitch and Ian Charlton, who first introduced us to mountain biking in the Lake District, and to Andy Stephenson, for his invaluable advice and endless supply of jam sandwiches.

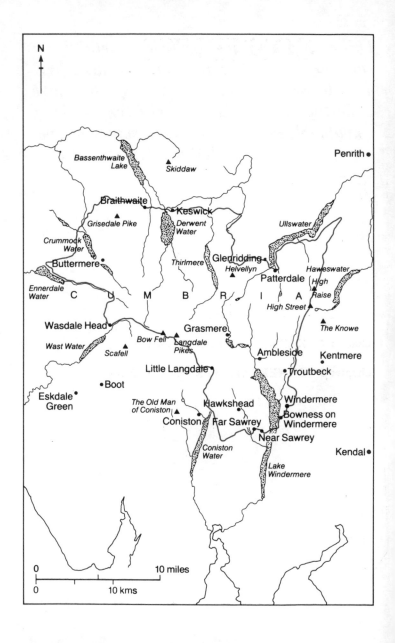

CONTENTS

About the book

There are a number of cycling books on the market which can tell you all about hub/gear ratios, freewheel sprockets and side-pull brakes. This isn't one of those books.

We're not expert mountain bikers in the normal sense: we couldn't tell you how to adjust your gears – we're not even much use at mending punctures.

Our only qualification for writing this book is that we like mountain biking – not using a mountain bike to nip down to the newsagent to pick up an evening paper, or simply to indulge in a bit of posing. We enjoy putting a mountain bike to the use for which it was originally intended.

This guide concentrates on the Lake District – but it is as much a guide to the pleasures of mountain biking as it is to the sights and scenery you will encounter en route.

The main part of the book is divided into seven chapters. In each of them you will find described one instalment in a complete, 100-mile circular route around the Lake District. You don't have to try to conquer the whole of the Lakes in one go – although this is possible if you are super fit, or mad. As well as listing the main sights and historical attractions en route – with information on some of the famous people connected with that region – we also suggest some other rides in the same area. There are low-level circuits, ascents of peaks and linking routes between valleys. In a sense this book is a jigsaw, with each ride described here another piece in the puzzle. We have put it together one way, but you can take it apart and create an entirely different picture. With this book, the appropriate Ordnance Survey maps and some imagination you could cycle off-road for weeks and never cover the same ground twice.

Each section also contains valuable service information about hotels, pubs, shops and cycle stores.

Our circuit runs anticlockwise from Windermere, but we also provide the information to enable you to start at Penrith, Keswick or just about anywhere else. You can also tackle the route clockwise if you wish, though because of the lie of the land you will not be taking full advantage of short, sharp ascents and long, rideable descents if you do so.

Whichever way you go, one thing is sure – you are certain to enjoy yourself. If you have a mountain bike, and have never used it off the main road, this book will offer you a good introduction.

We hope you have fun.

If you have comments on or suggestions for the book, please write to us at Lake District Mountain Bike Book, PO Box 67, Bath, Avon.

Andy Bull
Frank Barrett

Preface

It's not exactly an exhaustive survey of public opinion, but the British Rail guard who helped us load a bike on to a train at Paddington station probably summed up many people's feelings on the subject.

"That's an impressive-looking piece of expensive machinery," he said, and added sarcastically: "Twenty-one gears? Lightweight frame? I expect you go up a lot of mountains on that, don't you? I don't expect you go on it further than the pub."

It was a fair observation. Many people, including many who buy them, see mountain bikes as a sort of fashion accessory – "high street jewellery" to use one description. It looks good, it's expensive – and, almost as an afterthought, it's a useful means of transport around town.

Probably as many as half of the new bikes that are bought in Britain are mountain bikes – that's a million a year, a remarkable figure when you consider they have been available in this country for less than ten years.

Like most modern trends, mountain biking came out of America. About 15 years ago in Marin County, California, a bunch of post-hippy bike freaks developed a passion for riding down mountains on old-fashioned American bikes with balloon tyres. These lunatic races became popular and quickly attracted the attention of bike manufacturers – particularly the Japanese, who know a good thing when they see one.

From these early prototype machines, the mountain bike was born. It has rapidly become the most lucrative part of the retail bike trade and the mainstay of the city cycle messenger service business. But few mountain bike owners actually use their expensive, elegant machines to venture off the beaten track.

This is a great pity. The truth is that mountain bikes perform to their best ability off the metalled road (enthusiasts for conventional bikes dislike the heavy, energy-absorbing tyres of mountain bikes). A mountain bike only really comes into its own in the countryside – riding up a rough lane, where you have a chance to work through the whole range of gears. A mountain bike offers a unique chance to see the best of the British countryside.

But the idea of such "serious" mountain biking probably strikes the casual cyclist as a little too daunting. In fact "serious" mountain bikers in their cut-off trousers and crash helmets, with their trade talk of braised fillets and oversize headsets, don't look much like people keen to enjoy themselves. And mountain bikes appear to eschew the benefits of mudguards – "serious" mountain bikers seem to want to get wet and muddy.

Don't be put off. Part of the reason why we decided to write this series of mountain bike guides is to show that the whole business can be fun. To get the most pleasure out of mountain biking, you don't need mountains – although mountains can be fun. All you need is to find a route away from the main highways.

This isn't as difficult as you might think. The whole of Britain is criss-crossed with a huge network of tracks and paths, particularly bridleways, over which mountain bikes can be taken. Within an hour's drive of Charing Cross, for example, you can dump the car, hop on a mountain bike and find yourself deep in the heart of the wildest countryside.

You don't necessarily need cut-off shorts, or even a crash helmet – though you may find both more useful than you think. What you need is a sense of adventure and plenty of energy and enthusiasm.

But be warned: what starts as a pleasant pastime can quickly become a habit-forming obsession. After a few expeditions, you could soon find yourself at the bike shop drooling over light-weight frames and lasciviously eyeing the latest accessories. It's worth the risk . . .

Introduction

At last we were there. After an hour and a half of very hard climbing this was it: the summit of Helvellyn, at 3,113 ft the highest point in England where you can legally be on a mountain bike. As Cagney might have said: "Made it Ma! Top of the world."

If you believe in starting at the top, the ride up Helvellyn is the place to begin cycling in the Lake District. You will not be disappointed. As you lean against the summit marker on Helvellyn, grinning for the victory photograph, you can look forward to up to five hours of exhilarating ridge-top cycling ahead of you.

The views are stunning in every direction. To the north-west you can see the town of Keswick with Skiddaw and Bassenthwaite Lake beyond. South there is a glimpse of Windermere. East is Ullswater and the great whale's-back of the High Street range, which offers fantastic cycling almost from Windermere right up the length of the National Park to Penrith. West, on a clear day, you look out over the massed peaks to the Irish Sea.

From where you stand you can take a quick inventory of what the Lake District offers. There is every kind of off-road cycling here, from gentle perambulations around lakes to forest treks, pass routes which give quick links between valleys, and ascents of some of the highest summits in the country. Every level of experience, every degree of adventurousness, can be catered for.

You could have a great time cycling here without going for the high ground at all. But, we suggest, you will be missing a lot if you don't. Getting up Helvellyn – and any other mountain – is, admittedly, tough. Ascents vary in difficulty but on most of them you will have to carry the bike for a time. That might sound as if it rather defeats the object. It is supposed to be an All Terrain Bike, after all. The way we look at it is that if the rewards outweigh the effort involved in scrambling up a mountain then it is worth it. Helvellyn is certainly worth it, and your exertions will be quickly forgotten as you swoop north along the ridge. You judder over Raise, with its rocky summit looking like a moonscape, swoop down to Sticks Pass over rock covered with a layer of thick, soft vegetation which is just like cycling over a vast, wrinkled carpet and glide over grass as green as on any downland meadow as you tackle Stybarrow Dodd and Watson's Dodd.

From there you pick up an old, eighteenth-century coach road which arcs round to deliver you, via a couple of quiet lanes, to your starting-point. What could be better? It is important, however, not to over-reach yourself. To do so in a mountainous region where one must be aware of the hazards, not least the weather's potential to turn from the benign to the nasty in minutes, is asking for trouble. Getting on a mountain bike if you have not cycled for years and battling off up Helvellyn is unwise, to say the least. When Andy first swung his leg over a mountain bike it was in the Lake District, after a good lunch on a warm spring day. Urged on by a very experienced friend he belted bravely up Skiddaw. Within ten minutes he was exhausted, his legs felt as if they belonged to someone else and each breath seemed as if it were dragged through sand. But the increasing feeling of nausea was the most worrying symptom. He lost his lunch just after he lost his balance.

A year later he was back, fresh from a couple of months of regular cycling on the Ridgeway, which runs across central southern England from the Thames at Streatley to beyond Avebury in Wiltshire, and is written about in the companion volume to this one.

He thought he was more or less fit for anything the Lake District fells could throw at him. He wasn't. Tackling mountains meant becoming a beginner all over again. Even if the All Terrain Bike cannot conquer everything, it is still capable of a great deal more than the average cyclist. The process of learning to cycle in such country is an enlightening one. You match yourself against the machine, which can do most things, and gradually find your abilities grow to encompass more of the potential the bike offers.

How far you take it depends on you. Neither of us is addicted to physical challenges for their own sake. We will only climb a particular peak if there is a sufficient reward for having done so in terms of sustained, ridge-top cycling, a fantastic view or some magic connected with the place. Helvellyn rewards the mountain biker generously on all three counts.

The hard core among mountain bikers are looking for thrills and spills, excitement and an element of danger. We are not, and believe that the vast majority of mountain cyclists will be like us, keen to use the machine over the terrain it was designed for but also pretty keen to get home in one piece and well to this side of total exhaustion.

This book is designed for what might best be described as the fell cyclist: the person who, ideally, knows at least a little about what it is like up mountains, the skills you need, the dangers you must be aware of, but who wants to advance from being restricted to where his feet can take him in a day to the new, wider horizon created by the mountain bike.

The cyclist moves up a grade from footpaths, on which it is illegal to cycle, to bridleways. In the Lake District, many of the routes so designated are former packhorse routes which linked isolated valleys and brought, via the itinerant salesmen, their only links with the outside world. Others were used to transport ore from the once numerous lead, copper and other mines. There are the courses of Roman roads, coach roads and even coffin routes used to take the dead from remote communities to burial grounds. Such routes have not been used for their original purpose for many years, but all are open to the mountain biker. Cycling does a lot for you, physically. It is surprising how fit you can get in just a few days. Pushing the pedals gives you the thighs of an Adonis, while clinging grimly on to the brakes gives you the hands of a strangler – not to mention ailments such as mountain biker's knee, elbow, back and neck.

We worried initially about how welcome bikes would be on the fells. We expected some resentment from walkers, but found hardly any. In fact, taking a mountain bike up a mountain is like taking a smiling baby into an old people's home. Everyone makes a fuss, everyone wants one. When we were going up Helvellyn, plenty of people could see the advantage of having a mountain bike once you were at the top, but not all fancied doing the carrying. "That's it lads," went the often-heard joke, "carry them up, we'll take them from there."

The cyclists themselves are a fraternity, always stopping to discuss routes with each other, swap information on paths, bikes, or good and bad experiences on the fells. They will ask you where you are going and tell you the best way to get there. Many of their expeditions are taken half blind. They see a promising-looking bridleway on the map and go and try it. There is, in short, something of an information gap. We hope this book fills it.

The hardwear and the softwear

The mountain bike
The cynic would say a mountain bike is an ordinary bike with a fancy paint job for those with more money than sense. Well, they are certainly more expensive and are no doubt seen as fashion accessories by some. However, a mountain bike has essential characteristics that set it apart.

It is designed for off-road use and is consequently more robust than the average touring bike. To cope with steep ascents it has 15, 18 or 21 gears and, to cope with fast and steep descents, much stronger brakes. Its tyres are designed to maximise traction rather than minimise rolling resistance, so they are fat and knobbly rather than narrow and smooth.

History of the mountain bike
Mountain bikes were invented in Marin County, northern California, in the 1970s by a group with a penchant for bombing down dirt roads in forests and other remote places. No one was producing mountain bikes commercially at the time, and most machines were either hand-made to personal specifications or they were heavily refined production models.

They used old-fashioned, hefty, large-tubed frames, often 20, 30 or 40 years old, but combined them with the then state-of-the-art 10-speed gearing of racing bikes. At first the bikes were only ridden downhill and transported back en masse in pick-up trucks. Then someone had the bright idea of riding uphill as well as down.

The first custom-built mountain bike frame was commissioned by Charles Kelly, which has earned him the title "Father of the Mountain Bike". Mountain bike frames were manufactured commercially in 1979. And the rest, as they say, is history.

Buying a bike: where to buy
You would not buy a car from a department store, nor should you purchase a bike from one. A mountain bike is going to take some rough treatment. You should buy from a specialist shop. You need to be able to take it back if it goes wrong and deal with someone who knows all about the machines. If the salesman also sells microwaves and dishwashers he is not likely to know much about the intricacies of your complex, delicate gearing system.

Manufacturers do not often assemble bikes completely. Final setting-up is usually left to the shop. You want to be sure that this was done by a bicycle mechanic, not someone who is more at home with hi-fis and videos.

Make sure the person selling to you knows his product. It is more likely in a small shop that the salesperson is the owner. Question them closely on the differences between bikes, don't let them blind you with science. If they rabbit on about STI etc. pin them down to what it means, how it works, why you need it.

Make it quite clear you want a bike for off-road use. Ask about after-sales service. A conscientious shopkeeper who wants you as a regular customer should offer a free service after a month or so. By then everything will have bedded in and adjustments will be needed.

How much to spend
Mountain bikes do not differ greatly in essentials. Whatever surface distinction the exotic paint job may give, the machine beneath will probably have a frame and wheels made in Taiwan and a gearing and braking system from Japan.

The bike may have been designed in Europe or North America, but all but the most expensive will have been manufactured abroad. Often a bike will bear the wording:

"Hand built in England", which is no doubt true, but can mean simply that it arrived at the shop in bits and was hand built there.

Most manufacturers have a range of models, beginning with a basic bike at about £200, then going up in stages at roughly £300, £350, £400, £450, £650, £850 and on into the exotics at anything up to £2,000.

Decide how much you want to spend, then look for the bike that offers you the most for your money. The chances are you will find little to choose between competing models at a similar price. One of us narrowed our choice down to a Ridgeback and a Trek with a price difference of 20p. In terms of equipment they were identical. It was a toss-up which to buy.

Do not overlook details. One of us bought a bike with a foam-covered saddle. In wet weather it was not nice to sit on. The bike did not have a protective strip of metal or plastic to prevent the chain bouncing on it and chipping the paint. If you find two bikes with little between them in engineering terms, look for the details which indicate how thoughtful the manufacturer has been in kitting the bike out.

Mountain bike anatomy

All these technical terms can seem like a foreign language to the layman, but they will help you communicate with the oily characters in the bike shop.

First the frame. It's a triangle, almost, with the top tube at the top, the seat tube under the saddle and the down tube holding them together. The tube that prevents the frame from quite becoming a triangle is the head tube, which links the front forks – which hold the wheel – and the handlebars.

At the bottom of the seat tube and down tube is the bottom bracket, which holds the axle to which the pedal cranks are attached. The two or three chainrings here make up the chainset. The thing which makes the chain switch between these chainrings is the front derailleur. The springy thing which dangles down beside the rear wheel and through which the chain threads is the rear derailleur, which shifts the chain from one rear sprocket to another. The controls on the handlebars with which you change gear are the thumb shifters.

Now, from the phrases above you should be able to stroll into a bike shop and make up impressive sounding sentences such as: "I have just gone bottom bracket over top tube, buckling my chainset and catching my thumb shifter in my rear derailleur. Please help."

Cycling off-road

Equipment
Some go for the lot, some for none. As with fell-walking, there are those who set off in a pair of old shoes and a tatty Parka, others who kit themselves out in full, fluorescent outfits, expensive footwear, helmets, gloves, backpacks, plastic map cases, the lot.

There is a vast industry dedicated to turning out high-fashion clothing and other accessories for mountain bikers. How much gear, and how high-fashion is up to you. However, there are certain basic standards of equipment below which you are not safe off-road. Rough conditions require a certain amount of tough gear.

Fashionable, skin-tight cycle garb is not suitable for cycling in inclement conditions, because it does not conserve body heat. If you plan to cycle off-road for sustained periods, particularly in high country, you should ensure that you have clothes to keep you warm and dry in the worst conditions you might encounter. It is a good idea to wear several layers which you can peel off as you get hot and put on again as you cool off. Temperatures can drop dramatically when climbing – 3 °F per 1,000 ft is a fair average, which means that if you cycle up a 3,000-ft mountain the temperature is likely to drop 9 °F, more if weather conditions are adverse.

Footwear is a matter of taste. Trainers are light and comfortable, but if you are struggling over rough country you might prefer a light walking-boot.

The benefits of helmets are widely debated. Those in favour say they save lives, those against say that they encourage reckless behaviour because wearers feel safer when performing feats they would not consider without a helmet. All we can say is that, bouncing down a steep incline, ever conscious of the danger of being toppled over the handlebar by some rogue rock, we feel a lot safer in a helmet.

If you buy one make sure that it conforms to British Safety Standards. It should be as close-fitting as possible and worn with the chin-strap tightly fastened. Once you have taken a tumble in a helmet, replace it, even if it does not seem damaged. Helmets work by absorbing the blow of an impact; they do not work well unless in pristine condition.

A basic tool kit is essential. One of us learnt that by being faced with a time-wasting five-mile walk because he did not have a puncture kit with him when cycling the Ridgeway. Neat little packs which strap on beneath the saddle or to the frame are ideal. You will need a puncture repair kit, spanners, screwdriver and Allen keys, plus a pump and a tool for removing links from your chain.

If you take the bike up fells or mountains you will have to carry it for periods. To stop the bike's hard, unyielding frame doing unspeakable damage to your soft one, pad the frame so that the bike can be shouldered comfortably. A shoulder sling which attaches inside the frame beneath the saddle is ideal. You can then slip your arm through the frame, balancing the bike with your right hand on the handlebars. These slings often incorporate a small triangular tool bag.

It can be a problem puzzling how to mount pump and water-bottle in such a way as not to impede carrying. Some people prefer to carry everything in a rucksack. Again, this is a question of personal taste.

One of the most important pieces of equipment you will need is a bike-carrier for your car: there are now dozens of types of these available, from roof-rack types to those that attach to the back of your car. We both have hatchback cars and find the sort that attaches to the top of the back door and the bottom of the rear bumper the most handy (these cost from around £35 and normally carry up to three bikes). Take care that these do not obscure your rear number plate, or you will be breaking the law.

Navigation
Ordnance Survey maps, where available the large-scale 2.5 inch to the mile maps in the Outdoor Leisure series, are essential if

you are to avoid getting lost or wasting time in taking wrong routes. This book has been designed for use in conjunction with a good map. On sustained off-road routes you should also take a compass. In poor visibility it will be invaluable.

Getting lost can be extremely easy: much easier than you would ever have thought.

Fitness

Cycling is one of the best forms of exercise, but a long ride off-road will burn up a good deal of energy. Vigorous cycling, the sort you are likely to do plenty of on fells or downs, will burn up 7–10 calories a minute. Even after you have finished riding for the day, your metabolic rate remains high. You will feel warm for a couple of hours, and burn more calories because of it.

You must eat well, otherwise you will burn up your energy stores and your performance will suffer. Sensible, healthy eating is the key: plenty of high-fibre cereal, wholemeal bread, chicken, fish, raw vegetables, brown rice, pasta and fresh fruit.

Take high-energy snacks with you, and an adequate supply of water. If your body fluid level drops by as little as two per cent greater heat loss results and performance suffers.

A mountain biker's code
The Sports Council and the Countryside Commission have drawn up a code of conduct for mountain bikers to which we heartily subscribe. Essential guidelines are:

Fasten all gates.
Leave no litter.
Do not harm wildlife, trees or plants.
Keep to rights of way across farmland.
Use gates and stiles to cross fences, hedges and walls.
Leave livestock, crops and machinery alone.
Guard against fire risks.
Help to keep all water clean.
Keep dogs under control.
Make no unnecessary noise.

In addition, if mountain biking is to improve its image it is important that all cyclists avoid riding on public footpaths, where they have no legal right to be. Keep to bridleways, byways and green roads. On bridleways there is a public right to travel on horse or cycle.

Give way to walkers and horse riders and remember that local authorities have the right to ban cyclists from bridleways. Do not be the one who gives them an excuse to do so.

It also helps to be cheerful and polite. We make it a point to say "Hello" to everyone we meet on our travels (even if this merry greeting is met with the sort of look that suggests "Who is this cheerful lunatic on a pink bike . . . ?").

The landscape of the lakes

It was the poet William Wordsworth who, 180 years ago, described the Lake District as being like a great wheel, with the hub half-way between the peaks of Great Gable and Scafell and the valleys fanning out from this point like the spokes.

His comparison may not have been perfect, but it does serve as a very good model to help one visualise the geography of the Lake District.

The observer perched in the centre of Wordsworth's circle will be hovering somewhere just to the south of Derwent Water. If he looks first to the south-east, says Wordsworth, he will see the vale of Langdale, "which will conduct the eye to the long lake of Winandermere [Windermere], stretched nearly to the sea; or rather to the sands of the vast bay of Morecambe, serving here for the rim of this imaginary wheel".

Looking from south-east to south he will see the vale of Coniston which, unlike the other valleys, does not reach the hub and is therefore, reasons Wordsworth, rather like a broken spoke attached only at the rim end.

Next, moving west, is the vale of Duddon, which has no lake in it. It is followed in turn by Eskdale (which reaches the sea at Ravensglass), Wastdale, Ennerdale, the vale of Buttermere (with Crummock Water and Loweswater beyond), and Borrowdale, running north to Derwent Water and Keswick. To see the other half of the wheel, says Wordsworth, the observer must wing his way four or five miles east and perch above Helvellyn. From here, continuing to move clockwise, he will see St John's Vale, Ullswater (stretching due east), Haweswater and, lastly, the vale of Grasmere, Rydal and Ambleside.

The highest peaks are towards the centre of this circle, with the land gradually subsiding into gentle foothills the further from the hub one travels. Lines of communication have tended to be dictated by the lie of the land. But while the roads follow the valleys and necessitate journeys, often, up one spoke to the hub before you can drive down another one, the mountain biker is almost uniquely equipped to take to the hills, to travel into the heart of a landscape which Wordsworth characterised as moving, as one gets closer to the hub, "from elegance and richness to grandeur and sublimity". The land, he goes on "encompasses every possible embellishment of beauty, dignity and splendour, which light and shadow can bestow upon objects so diversified . . . I do not know any tract of country in which, within so narrow a compass, may be found an equal variety in the influences of light and shadow upon the sublime or beautiful features of landscape."

The making of the landscape
Three distinct types of rock have created three shadings of character in the Lakes. In the north and south are two types of sedimentary rock, between them volcanic material. The north is made up of an Ordovician rock, formed between 440 and 500 million years ago and known locally as Skiddaw Slates. This rock is rather dull in colour and creates smooth, rounded hills. Close up, it makes Skiddaw itself look like the biggest slag heap in the world.

In the south is Silurian rock, formed between 400 and 440 million years ago. Again this causes a rounded landscape, but has a distinctive greeny tinge which is instantly recognisable in the buildings.

The Igneous rock in between, and around Wordsworth's hub, is harder and has created the high, jagged peaks of central lakeland such as the Scafell Pikes.

But it was the Ice Age, 2 million years ago, that saw glaciers ploughing down from the hub and gouging out the valleys, leaving the peaks exposed and creating the huge ruts in which the lakes formed. Add to that millennia of frost, rain and wind (plus a few years of man, with his big boots and knobbly tyres) and there you have it: the Lake District.

Nature
There are Golden Eagles in the Lake District, though you can count yourself lucky to see one. They have been spotted above the Straits of Riggindale, on the High Street range in eastern lakeland. Golden Eagles, which can have a wing-span of up to 7 ft and hunt for rabbits, hares and grouse, build their eyries on high, rocky ledges.

Buzzards are fairly common. They feed on rabbits and other small mammals and carrion. In spring, pairs may be seen spiralling upwards, the male then diving on the female. The buzzard's call is a distinctive, plaintive mewing. Ravens, the largest member of the crow family, nest on crags and eat carrion as well as killing small animals and taking eggs.

Lapwings, with their distinctive "pee-wit" call, are often heard over areas of heath in the Lake District. The small black, white and dark green birds make their nests on the ground.

Another frequenter of upland moors is the Golden Plover. In spring the yellow-spangled birds can be seen flitting over their territory and climbing to a great height. The cry is a mournful note that can make a desolate place seem even lonelier.

Plant life
On the peaks lichen and moss are the prevalent ground cover, while further down the fells, grasses such as Sheep's Fescue and Purple Moor Grass are common. Alpine flowers are often found, as their spreading habit makes them better able to survive winds that might dislodge anything taller.

Rowan and birch often get a foothold in steep slopes where sheep cannot get at them. Bilberry is found on areas of shallow peat, with heather covering the drier moors. In wet areas, sphagnum and other mosses are common. Bracken is estimated to cover a good 10 per cent of the uplands and is a bane to the cyclist, twisting round pedals and jamming wheels.

To see upland wildlife in abundance it is a good idea to move along the banks of a mountain stream, where you are likely to see a good range of grasses, ferns and mosses. Primroses thrive in sheltered conditions. In spring, wild daffodils carpet the lowlands, especially on the shores of Ullswater, where Wordsworth saw the golden host about which he wrote.

Classification of routes in this book

Each route is graded 1 to 5 in terms of difficulty: Grade 1 routes should be within the scope of a complete novice; routes get progressively harder until Grade 5 rides, which involve tough cycling (including ascents to summits or other challenging terrain).

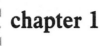

chapter 1

WINDERMERE to HIGH STREET

Towns: Windermere, Troutbeck and Kentmere
Lakes: Windermere, Haweswater

Introduction to the area

For many of its 19 million annual visitors, the Lake District begins at Windermere, which is far from being the best advertisement for the place. If you approach from the south, road and rail will deliver you here. Windermere is a sort of transit camp, full of people in a hurry to get somewhere else. Just down the road is Bowness-on-Windermere, its ugly little runt of a brother, and a sort of mini-Blackpool-by-the-lake.

The good news is that, with a mountain bike, you can leave Windermere for the real countryside as fast as you like. Go north, and you are in the silent, green, upper reaches of Troutbeck within minutes. Go west, and the Bowness ferry spirits you to the far bank of Windermere, and a complete contrast to the gaudy tat five minutes behind you across the water.

If you plan to complete the full 100-mile (160-km) Lake District circuit described in this book, and are to travel anticlockwise, Chapter 1 takes you north over High Street which, confusingly, is not just the name of a mountain. It is also the name of a Roman road, the route they used to link their garrisons at Ambleside and Penrith.

Today there is little evidence of it left, but its course runs true to form, powering straight up High Street (the mountain) to 2,663 ft (811 m) before running along the great hog's-back of a ridge right up past Pooley Bridge, at the very top of Ullswater, to the far end of the Lake District.

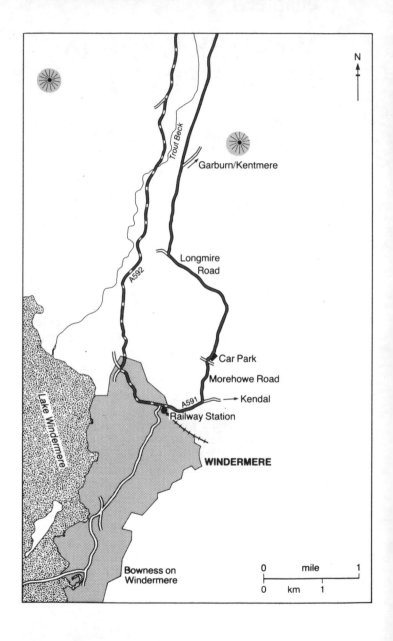

N

Trout Beck

Garburn/Kentmere

Longmire
Road

A592

Car Park

Morehowe Road

A591   → Kendal

Railway Station

WINDERMERE

Lake Windermere

Bowness on
Windermere

0	mile	1
0	km	1

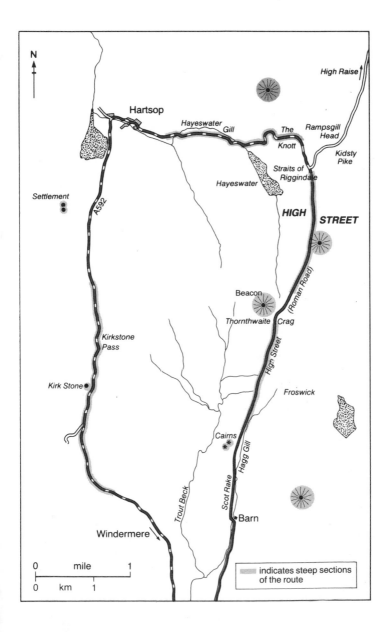

N

High Raise

Hartsop

Hayeswater Gill

The Knott

Rampsgill Head

Kidsty Pike

Straits of Riggindale

Hayeswater

Settlement

A592

HIGH STREET

Kirkstone Pass

Beacon

Thornthwaite Crag

(Roman Road)

High Street

Kirk Stone

Froswick

Cairns

Hagg Gill

Trout Beck

Scot Rake

Barn

Windermere

| 0 | mile | 1 |
| 0 | km | 1 |

indicates steep sections of the route

If you prefer to ride clockwise, the route takes you on the ferry across Lake Windermere towards Grizedale Forest. The latter is the easy way to begin, and perhaps advisable for the complete novice. Or you might like to stay within the area until you get the feel of the bike. The routes running to Kentmere and from the foot of Haweswater are a good place to learn, offering a little of just about everything you are likely to find touring the Lake District. This, incidentally, is also a very quiet area, overlooked by most visitors who belt along the main roads between Windermere, Ambleside and Keswick. And, while Windermere is the busiest lake, Haweswater is among the quietest. If you wish to move quickly into central lakeland, there is an easy, enjoyable route from Troutbeck over the hills to Ambleside.

The route

The first 9.6 miles (15.4 km), via Troutbeck and High Street Roman road.

Ascent of 722 yds over 3 miles (660 m over 4.8 km) from Troutbeck to High Street.
No descents.
2.4 miles (3.8 km) on metalled roads.
Grade 4.

From Windermere railway station turn right and travel east on the A591 for half a mile (0.8 km). First left leads to Moorhouse Road. Turn left and, after half a mile (0.8 km), look out for Longmire Road, where the off-road cycling begins, on the right. Cars can be parked here.

For the next five miles (8 km) the route is a flat farm track running in the narrow valley cut by Troutbeck, and later Hagg Gill, between the fells. The only junction comes after one mile off-road (1.6 km), when the Garburn Road peels off to the right. Keep straight on. This is also the point where the old Roman road joins the route, from the left. Cross from the right to the left bank of the stream at a bridge beside a barn.

When open fell is reached the route runs uphill, steeply at first, in a groove called Scot Rake. The path runs to the left (just to west of north), to avoid running straight up the face of the fell.

Climbing steadily, it joins the ridge route between Froswick and Thornthwaite Crag. As you approach the 14-ft high pillar of stones built on the latter's summit, the path swings right (north-east) and heads straight for High Street itself, running just to the right (east) of the summit, on which there is an Ordnance Survey column.

In the dip beyond High Street the path forks. To the left is the path to The Knott, from which one can descend to Patterdale. To continue along the ridge north go right along the path heading for Kidsty Pike. After 150 yds (137 m), at the top of Rampsgill Head, turn left, where an indistinct path runs over grass to join the main route heading for the next peak, High Raise.

What you will see

On the main route: Thornthwaite Crag (2,569 ft or 783 m) is made distinctive by the 14-ft high stone column or beacon built on its summit. The best views are south-west across Windermere. Almost the whole of the lake, the largest in England, can be seen. Its vital statistics are: 10.5 miles long, 1 mile wide and 219 ft deep (16.8 km by 1.6 km by 67 m). It has been used for centuries as a water highway, transporting everything from Roman troops to iron ore. Today there are many pleasure boats.

High Street (2,718 ft or 828 m) is also known as Racecourse Hill. In past centuries local farmers and shepherds met here each year on 10 July. Ostensibly they got together to return sheep which had strayed and become attached to other flocks, but the occasion was also one for celebration, a feast, and games. On the broad, flat summit they would eat a meal, accompanied by ale, the barrels having been rolled up the fells. There was fox-hunting, wrestling, running and jumping but the main attraction was horse racing.

There are superb views from the summit. South is the Troutbeck valley, the southern half of Windermere and, on a good day, Morecambe Bay. Six miles (9.6 km) to the west is the Helvellyn range. North-west is Hayeswater reservoir. East is Blea Water tarn and, beyond it, the southern end of Haweswater reservoir, which has a wide, white tidemark when the water level is low.

Haweswater was only turned into a reservoir in the late 1930s, to supply Manchester. In the process the village of Mardale Green was cleared and flooded. Four farms, a school, cottages and a pub called the Dun Bull are under the lake. The church of Holy Trinity was dismantled in 1936 and the stones used to help build the reservoir. There was once a much smaller lake, 2.5 miles (4 km) long instead of the four miles (6.4 km) of today, at the north end of the valley. A dam 1,550 ft wide and 90 ft high (470 m by 27 m) was built and the water level raised by 96 ft (29 m). At its deepest the lake is 198 ft (60 m).

The village is under the southern end of the lake, just on the shoulder around The Rigg from the car park. The dry-stone walls which once enclosed the lane running to the southern end of the valley can still be seen disappearing into the water and, in periods of drought (the last was in 1984), the buildings emerge from the depths, together with the hump-backed Chapel Bridge which took the lane over Mardale Beck. So many people flocked to see it in 1984 that roads to the valley had to be closed.

Ironically, 100 years ago Mardale sent 3,000 lb of butter to Manchester a week; now it supplies thousands of gallons of water. They'd never get away with such destruction today. Would they?

One virtue of the reservoir is that the area is even quieter and more remote-seeming than it must have been when it was inhabited. Golden Eagles have returned to this corner of the Lake District. You might just see them when you are on the ridges, perhaps at the Straits of Riggindale.

In the area: Most of the routes used later in this chapter are ancient roads. There was probably once a highway crossing lakeland from the west coast at Ravenglass and running through Eskdale to Ambleside, on to Troutbeck, then following the Garburn Road and the crossing from Kentmere to Longseddale, (both used in routes described later in this chapter) and ending up at Shap. Today the M6, A6 and main London–Glasgow railway all use the north–south pass that the track would have encountered there.

The Nan Bield Pass used in the Haweswater-Kentmere circuit is an ancient trading route linking the villages of Mardale Green and Kentmere.

Famous connections

Arthur Ransome used Windermere, together with Coniston, as settings for his book *Swallows and Amazons*, the archetypally English adventures of a bunch of kids messing about in boats. In 1924 he bought a house up in the hills a mile (1.6 km) from the eastern shore of Windermere and five miles (8 km) south of Bowness. He wrote of it:

We have found a cottage, on very high ground but sheltered from the north, overlooking the whole valley of the Whinster. From the terrace in front of the house you can see Arnside and a strip of sea under the Knott. Away to the left you can see Ingleborough, and from the fell just behind the house you can see Ambleside, and all the lake hills. The house is called Low Ludderburn and is marked on the Ordnance Maps.

Here, Ransome sat down to write, quoting Walter Scott, "a book that a child shall understand, yet a man will feel some temptation to peruse should he chance to take it up". The five children of some neighbours were given two 14 ft dinghies which Ransome helped them sail. One was named *Swallow*, the other *Mavis*; *Swallow* was their favourite. From the experience of pleasant days on the water Ransome crafted a story which he hoped would capture the magic of boats, lakes and islands.

Hugh Brogan (writing in *The Life of Arthur Ransome*, Jonathan Cape 1974) said that, in the book: "the children would come to the shores of the lake, find *Swallow*, and then an island, and then go exploring further. And like all explorers they would meet adventurers: pirates; savages."

Turning the route into a circuit

Descent from the Straits of Riggindale via The Knott and Hayeswater: 13 miles (20.8 km).

Descent of 616 yds over 2.5 miles (560 m over 4 km) from The Knott to Hartsop.

Ascent of 325 yds over 3.2 miles (295 m over 5 km) at Kirkstone Pass.

Descent of 310 yds over 3.6 miles (283 m over 5.7 km) from Kirkstone Pass.

10.5 miles (16.8 km) on metalled roads.

Grade 4.

Instead of proceeding to High Raise, take the right fork in the path at the Straits of Riggindale which curves round to The Knott and then goes over the ridge to the left and descends in a series of zig-zags to the outlet stream from Hayeswater. Cross the stream and descend the track to the left of it. At the bottom of the hill the path fords the stream and runs down to the A592. Turn left on it and cycle south over Kirkstone Pass back to Windermere.

Other routes in the area

Circuit from Windermere via Kentmere: 13.2 miles (21 km).
Ascent of 270 yds over 3 miles (250 m over 4.8 km) from Moorhowe Road.
Descent of 270 yds over 1.5 miles (250 m over 2.4 km) to Kentmere.
Ascent of 55 yds over 2.5 miles (50 m over 4 km) from Kentmere.
4.4 miles (7 km) on metalled road.
Grade 3.

From Windermere take the A591 east for half a mile (0.8 km), then the first lane left which brings you to Moorhowe Road. Turn left and first right, on to a track called Longmire Road.

After a mile (1.6 km), where another route crosses the track, take the right fork, called Garburn Road. After approximately another two miles (3 km) the route reaches the summit at Garburn and begins a quick descent down Garburn Pass. The descent is treacherous, strewn with heavy, loose boulders and often under water.

When you meet a lane, turn left into Kentmere, turning right opposite the church down the drive to Kentmere Hall. In front of the Hall turn left, open the gate and take the bridleway that leads through a field. The path climbs behind a wood back on to the fells. When the track used by farm vehicles veers right be sure to keep close to the dry stone wall on your left. At Park Beck, 1.5 miles (2.4 km) from Kentmere Hall, the path divides. Go across the river, not to the left. The path runs over soft turf and is often indistinct.

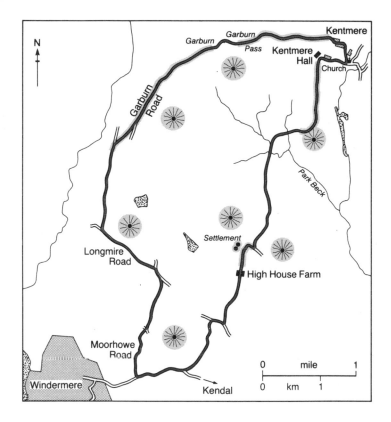

After 1.25 miles (2 km) you go through a gate to find a T-junction. To the left the path runs between dry-stone walls. Go right, climbing half-way across a field, and go through the gate to the left. This track leads down to High House farm. Go right in the farmyard then follow the tarmacked route to the Moorhowe Road. Turn right, first left and right onto the A591 for Windermere.

NB Linking the above route with the following one creates a full and very varied day's cycling, linking Windermere and Haweswater in a figure-of-eight.

Circuit from Haweswater via Kentmere: 11.5 miles (18.4 km).
Ascent of 400 yds in 1.6 miles (370 m over 2.5 km) from
Haweswater to Nan Bield Pass.
Descent of 400 yds in 2.2 miles (370 m over 3.5 km) from top of
Nan Bield Pass.
Ascent of 370 yds over 1.6 miles (340 m over 2.6 km) from
Kentmere to Gatesgarth Pass.
Descent of 350 yds over 1 mile (318 m over 1.6 km) from
Gatesgarth Pass to Haweswater.
Negligible distance on metalled roads.
Grade 5.

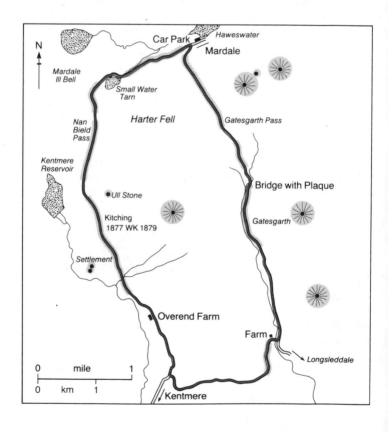

This is a tough but rewarding circuit which can be begun from either Haweswater or Kentmere and taken either clockwise or anticlockwise. Whichever way you do it, there will be one very steep, hard but safe ascent. We recommend going anticlockwise from Haweswater because that way you get the toughest climb, Nan Bield Pass, over with right at the start.

From the car park at the southern tip of Haweswater take the bridleway to the right of Harter Fell, signposted "Kentmere". There is a steep, rocky, but easily manageable climb to Small Water tarn. The path crosses the outlet stream and runs around the north shore. At the foot of Mardale Ill Bell it passes several very sound-looking rock shelters which date from the time when this was a packhorse route.

From here the climb is unrelenting until the top of Nan Bield Pass is reached. At the ridge is a right-angled shelter, and a ridge route running (left) to Harter Fell and (right) to Mardale Ill Bell. The path runs straight ahead down into Kentmere, zig-zagging steeply at first, then levelling out a good deal to give fast, easy riding right down to Kentmere. To the right as you descend is Kentmere reservoir. Just as you come level with its southernmost point the path crosses a rock on which is engraved "J KITCHING 1877" and, in a box, "WK 1879".

A lower track runs parallel to the route in the last stages, but stay on the higher path until Overend Farm, where the routes merge. Go left and follow the bridleway sign you see soon after the buildings. Soon after the road becomes metalled a bridleway sign marked "Longsleddale" points to the left. This takes you east into the next valley. After a mile (1.6 km) the track drops to a farm and runs over a bridge to a lane. Turn left for the climb to Gatesgarth. For a good two miles the gradient is easy, but there follows a steep climb up a newly-laid rock path which is too steep for most to cycle over.

After a gate onto the open fell there is a small bridge with, beneath its arch, a plaque reading "Denys Beddard 1917–1985". Soon after, the path divides. Follow the sign to Mardale via Gatesgarth Pass. The going is flat but boggy for a while, until another zig-zagging climb to the top of the pass. The descent begins steep and rocky, but relents after a while and the last mile (1.6 km) back to Haweswater is very pleasant.

Link from Troutbeck to Ambleside: 2.8 miles (4.5 km).
Ascent of 100 yds over 0.5 miles (90 m over 0.8 km) from
Troutbeck to junction with Hundreds Road.
Descent of 87 yds over 0.6 miles (80 m over 1 km) from junction
with Hundreds Road to Low Skelghyll.
Ascent of 32 yds over 0.4 miles (30 m over 0.65 km) from Low
Skelghyll to High Skelghyll.
Descent of 142 yds over 1.2 miles (130 m over 2 km) from High
Skelghyll to Ambleside.
Negligible stretch on metalled road.
Grade 2.

This is probably the route which the Roman road of High Street
took in its final swing around the top of Windermere to Galava,
the garrison at Ambleside.

Take the Bridleway called Robin lane, which leaves the village
to the left of the Post Office. After climbing for half a mile
(0.8 km) on a good farm track the path drops in the central
section, leaving the track for a narrow path across grass through
a gate to the left just after the summit. At the bottom of the hill
turn right to cross a bridge and climb up the farm track to High
Skelghyll. Go through the farmyard to a gate beyond the house.
Shortly after this the route begins its long, swift descent down
Skelghyll Lane through woods to Old Lake Road, emerging
opposite a car park. Go through the car park and turn right on
to the A591 for Ambleside town centre.

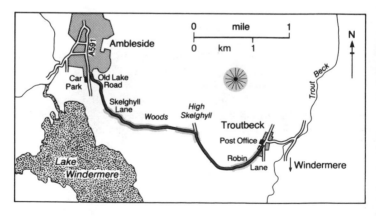

Facilities in Windermere

Windermere and Bowness-on-Windermere combined are the largest town in the Lake District. There is a reasonable range of shops, including a Booths Supermarket, with free car park, up behind the railway station.

Food and drink

Miller Howe Kaff, Lakeland Plastics, Station Precinct, Windermere. Tel. (09662) 2255.

Porthole Eating House, Ash Street, Bowness. Tel. (09662) 2793.

Jackson's Bistro, St Martin's Square, Bowness. Tel. (09662) 6264.

Rastelli, Lake Road, Bowness. Tel. (09662) 4277.

Porthole Vegetarian Restaurant, Lake Road, Bowness. Tel. (09662) 5002.

Hole Int' Wall, Lowside, Bowness on Windermere. Tel. (09662) 3488.

Grey Walls Hotel, Elleray Road, Windermere. Tel. (09662) 3741.

Accommodation

South Lakeland Where To Stay guide details hotels, guest houses, bed-and-breakfast, self-catering and caravan and camping sites for the area covered in this chapter. It is available from tourist information centres, or from South Lakeland District Council, Woolpack Yard, Kendal, Cumbria LA9 4NG, Tel. (0539) 733333.

Particularly when travelling in remote areas, Youth Hostels can be hugely convenient places to stay. The Youth Hostels Association has 19 within the area covered in this book, including one at High Close, Bridge Lane, Troutbeck; Tel. (09662) 3543. For a free leaflet called *Youth Hostels in Lakeland* send an sae to YHA, Bowey House, William Street, South Gosforth, Newcastle upon Tyne NE3 1SA.

Bikes

Biketreks: bike hire, guided rides, sales, spares, repair. A mobile service – they come to you. Tel. (05395) 31835; mobile phone (0860) 674171.

Staveley (four miles east of Windermere on the A591) has Lakeland Mountain Bikes. Sales, repair and hire. Shop: Low Green, Staveley. Tel. (0539) 821748. Hire section: Elterwater, Great Langdale, Nr Ambleside, just off the B5343.

Lakeland Leisure, Station Precinct, Windermere. Sales, hire.
Tel. (09662) 4786.
Tourist Information Centre
Victoria Street. Tel. (09662) 6499.

TROUTBECK
Post office selling some provisions.
Queens Head Hotel. Tel. (05394) 32174.
The Mortal Man. Tel. (05394) 33195.

chapter 2

HIGH STREET to PATTERDALE

Towns and villages: Penrith, Pooley Bridge
Lakes: Ullswater, Haweswater

Introduction to the area

Here are some of the finest but bleakest fells and one of the
prettiest lakes.

The High Street range dominates the whole eastern half of the
Lake District. If you don't ride it you will regret it. It will sit
there, like the biggest rebuke in the world, its huge whale-like
form visible from almost anywhere else you go. Look across from
some other, more glamorous, summit and there it will be:
unconquered, making your mountain biking incomplete.

Up there is wild, high moorland – nearly 2,700 ft (800 m) high
in the south, dropping steadily northwards to 1,000 ft (300 m) at
the most northerly point of this section of the Lake District round
trip. It is great – but lonely – cycling country. The only living
creatures you see all day may well be the semi-wild ponies that
make this their home – hardy-looking beasts with long, thick
manes and great, hairy feet. High Street has a bleakness you
might expect to find on Dartmoor. There are great areas of peat
like a giant grow-bag split open and spilled. Elsewhere the
heather-covered land drops two feet without warning in a step
that is almost invisible until you are right upon it.

A. Wainwright, writing in *The Far Eastern Fells*, Book 2 in his
Pictorial Guide to the Lakeland Fells, highlighted the area's
loneliness and urged more people to sample its pleasures:

"Rarely did I meet anyone on my explorations of the High Street fells", he wrote.

Usually I walked from morning till dusk without a sight of human beings. This is the way I like it, but what joys have been mine that other folk should share! Let me make a plea for the exhilarating hills . . . they should not remain neglected. To walk upon them, to tramp the ridges, to look from their tops across miles of glorious country, is constant delight. The Far Eastern Fells are for strong walkers and should please the solitary man of keen observation and imagination.

The area has another side, too. There is first-rate low-level cycling around Ullswater. This is one of the prettiest, and least spoilt of all the lakes. It was on its shores that William Wordsworth "wandered lonely as a cloud" (or "cow" as we like to believe the first draft read) and spotted those famous daffodils.

The route

17 miles (27.2 km).
Minor ascents.
Overall descent of 710 yds over 7.5 miles (650 m over 12 km).
No metalled roads.
Grade 1.

If you wish to join the route at this point, see the link route from Hartsop via The Knott described later in this chapter.

High Street Roman road crosses High Raise, passing 100 yds west of the summit cairn, before becoming enclosed between a dry-stone wall on the right and a fence on the left and running north-north-east to Raven Howe, where the wall and fence fall back on either side. Keep to the top of the ridge.

The path passes a few yards to the right of the cairn on Red Crag, before crossing Keasgill Head and Wether Hill. Half-way between this summit and the next, Loadpot Hill, the path divides. Take the left fork. The ruins of Lowther House, now little more than a pile of rubble and a concrete floor, are passed as the path swings left to skirt Loadpot Hill. The way is indistinct here, but the trigonometry point on the summit of Loadpot Hill is a good marker.

The path widens to cart width and begins the final, fast descent. Where the path divides, go right. The left fork runs across Arthur's Pike to the corner of Barton Park, but is not a bridleway. Just before the ford over Elder Beck, which runs in a deep gully, turn sharp left on to a clear grassy path which descends to run along at the top of Barton Park wood. After fording another stream in a gully the route picks up a dry-stone wall which it follows for three miles (4.8 km) or so before reaching a gate at a house called Mellguards, where a metalled drive runs down through Howtown to a lane. Turn left on the lane and at the junction turn right, signposted "Sandwick". Turn right at the second junction. The bridleway which turns off to the left near the end of the lane runs alongside Ullswater, about 50 yards (45 m) above the shore until coming parallel with the village of Patterdale. Here, a path descends, passes through a gate and joins a lane. Turn left and then right and join the A592 just south of the village.

If you are cycling this section of the route in isolation and began at Hartsop, turn left on the A592 and travel south for 1.5 miles (2.4 km) to regain your starting point.

What you will see

On the main route: Looking east from the High Street range you can see beyond Haweswater to the Pennines, looking west the Helvellyn range and Skiddaw. High Raise (2,634 ft or 802 m), second highest of the fells to the east of Ullswater and the Kirkstone Pass, is the last mountain as you travel north. After that there are really just rolling foothills. Occasionally you find red deer here which have strayed up from Martindale, the valley to the west.

There used to be a house just to the south of the summit of Loadpot Hill. Now it is a barely recognisable ruin. It was called Lowther House and was built as a shooting lodge with stables. You might make out the old fireplace though until 30 years ago the chimney stood and is still marked on the Ordnance Survey 2.5 inch maps.

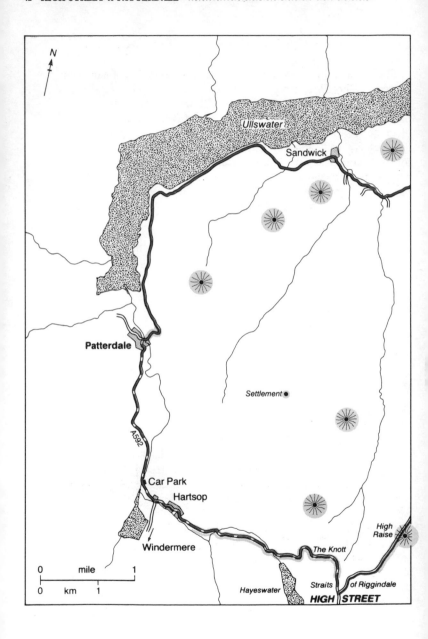

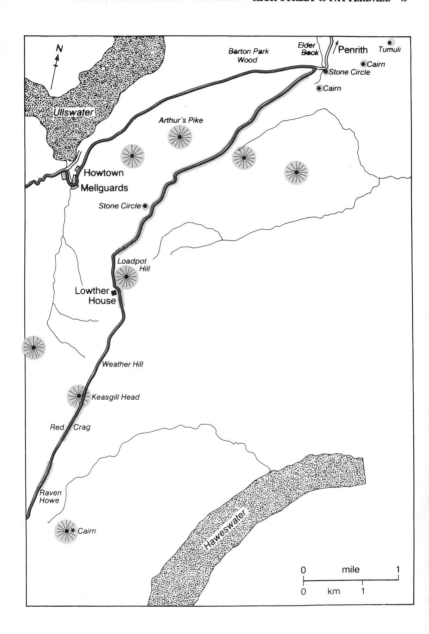

By the ford over Elder Beck, where the main route doubles back to the south, is the Cock Pit, where cock fights were once held.

In the area: At Boredale Hause, the pass at which routes for Patterdale, Martindale and Boredale converge, is a pile of stones which is all that remains of what is said to have been a chapel. It seems a particularly unlikely place to build one, but it is supposed to have been built here to serve the two communities of Patterdale and Boredale.

Ullswater is many people's favourite lake. It snakes for 7.5 miles (12 km) north from Patterdale to Pooley Bridge. On the way the landscape changes from the towering crags of the Helvellyn range to the gently rolling foothills of northern lakeland. The lake measures 0.75 miles (1.2 km) at its widest point and is up to 205 ft (65 m) deep.

Famous connections

William Wordsworth and his sister Dorothy saw the daffodils that inspired the famous poem "Daffodils" on the western shores of Ullswater:

"I wandered lonely as a cloud
*   That floats on high o'er vales and hills,*
When all at once I saw a crowd,
*   A host, of golden daffodils;*
Beside the lake, beneath the trees,
Fluttering and dancing in the breeze,"

He saw "ten thousand . . . at a glance" and, if you come in April or May you will still see the shore carpeted with *narcissus pseudonarcissus*, the wild lakeland variety.

Aira Force on the west shore just north of the A5091, is the setting for Wordsworth's poem "The Somnambulist".

Turning the route into a circuit

This is best done by starting at Hartsop, at the southern end of the Patterdale valley (see route description immediately below).

Other routes in the area

Link from Hartsop to High Street Roman road via Hayeswater: 2.5 miles (4 km).
Ascent of 616 yds over 2 miles from Hartsop to The Knott (560 m over 3 km).
No descents.
Negligible stretch on metalled road.
Grade 4.

From the car park on the A592 take the main road south for a few hundred yards and then turn left on the track running up to the fells. At a stream, where the track divides, take the right fork and ascent to Hayeswater reservoir. Here the path crosses to the left over a footbridge and climbs The Knott by a series of zigzags. At the ridge is a wall. Turn right and the path runs south-south-east to join the main route at the Straits of Riggindale. Turn left here.

Circuit from Howtown via Boredale Hause: 7 miles (11.2 km).
Ascent of 210 yds over 2 miles (190 m over 3.2 km) from Martindale to Boredale Hause.
Descent of 225 yds over 1.6 miles (205 m over 2.6 km) from Boredale Hause to Boredale.
4 miles (6.4 km) on metalled roads.
Grade 3.

From the car park just before the junction of lanes to Martindale and Sandwick turn south. Where the lane divides, keep left towards Martindale. Ride right to the end of the lane, at Dale Head farm. From here the path climbs up the side of Martindale Common on a wide, grassy but stone-strewn shelf.

There are fantastic views during the ascent into the wide bowl at the top of the dale, encircled by Rest Dodd, The Nab and other peaks which form a 1,500-ft to 1,800-ft (500 to 600-m) curtain to the south.

After two miles (3 km) of ascent the way levels out and you are on the broad, flat grassy top. The path runs left to Boredale Hause, a fell-top junction with routes down to Hartsop in the south, Patterdale to the west and our route, a right turn which takes us north-east down into Boredale. The descent is easy, on

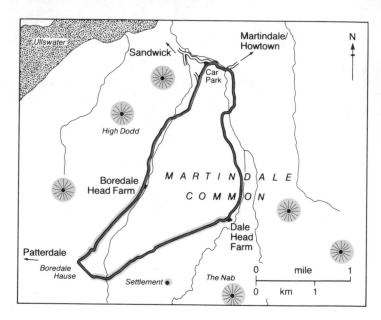

a wide, grassy shelf, except for a run of rough, loose and treacherous rock a few hundred yards down from the summit. At a farm called Boredale Head the road becomes metalled. Turn right when the lane forks and go straight on at the second junction, where our outward-bound route to Martindale goes off to the right. The starting-point is just beyond this turning.

Circuit from Pooley Bridge via Howtown: 9.2 miles (14.8 km).
Ascent of 180 yds over 1.8 miles (162 m over 2.9 km).
Descent of 186 yds over 3.6 miles (170 m over 5.8 km).
4 miles (6.4 km) on metalled roads.
Grade 1.

Leave Pooley Bridge on the lane heading east beside the church. After a crossroads (go straight on) the lane becomes a track and runs up on to the fells. At a crossroads after about a mile and a half (2.4 km) turn right, crossing a stream in a deep gully and travelling south-west, picking up a clear grassy path which descends to run along at the top of Barton Park wood. After

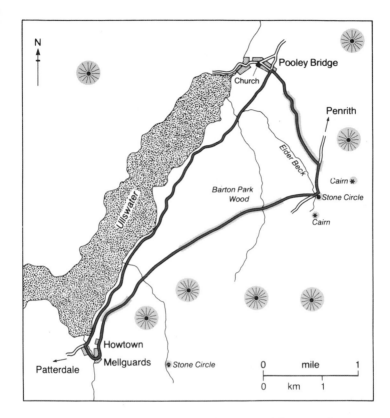

fording another stream in a gully the route picks up a dry-stone wall which it follows for three miles (4.8 km) or so before reaching a gate at a house called Mellguards where a metalled drive runs down through Howtown to a lane.

Turn right and follow the lane for four miles (6.4 km) before turning left and returning to Pooley Bridge.

Lakeside circuit from Patterdale: 3.6 miles (5.8 km).
Ascent of 80 yds over 0.2 miles (70 m over 0.4 km).
Descent of 80 yds over 1 mile (70 m over 1.6 km).
Negligible distance on metalled roads.
Grade 2.

For a low-level test of a mountain bike's mettle, this route cannot be beaten.

Take the lane at the southern end of the village, just past the Crown Inn. There are signposts here to Angle Tarn and Boredale Hause. At the T-junction go through the gate straight ahead, turn left and climb up the few yards to the path. Where the way forks at the site of an old quarry take the lower path. The path is rock-strewn and there are several steep descents over loose ground. After rounding Silver Point watch for a boulder-strewn path climbing steeply through a gully to your right.

Having clambered up this gully you come out on to a boggy pass running behind Silver Crag. The path then runs back along the fellside with the lower path visible below. If anything, it is even more bumpy and treacherous. Ignore the first path linking the two levels; your path descends to join the lower one just before the gate which leads back to the lane and Patterdale.

Link to Penrith: 7.5 miles (12 km).
No notable ascents or descents.
The majority on metalled roads.
Grade 1.

From the railway station turn left into Cromwell Road then follow the one-way system as it turns right into Brunswick Road. At the bottom you are forced to go left to circle Stricklandgate before cycling down Middlegate, which leads into Devonshire

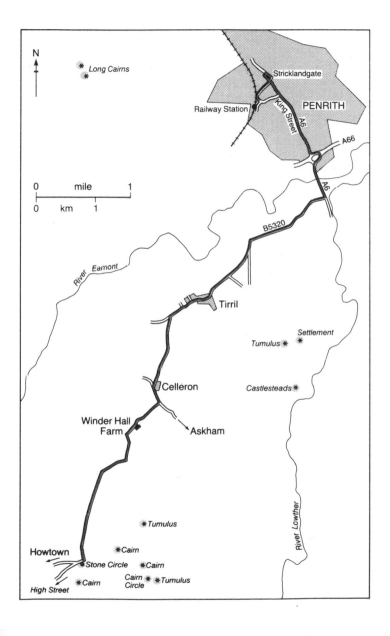

Road and King Street. You are now travelling south-east on the A6. Continue over the roundabout and take the first right, the B5320. Go through Tirril and take the first left, signposted "Celleron". At the next junction go left again, signposted "Askham and Haweswater". After a couple of hundred yards a bridleway, signposted "High Street", goes to the right, down the track to Winder Hall Farm. Past the farm, two tracks run across the rough grass and heather. The clearest runs uphill to the left and joins a more distinct path. Turn right here and when the path divides take the left fork and drop down to a bridleway crossroads. Go straight on, fording a river in a gully. On the other side two paths lie ahead. The one to the right leads down to Howtown beside Ullswater; to the left is the route south to High Street.

Link to Pooley Bridge: 1.8 miles (2.9 km).
Descent of 180 yds over 1.8 miles (162 m over 2.9 km).
Negligible stretch on metalled road.
Grade 1.

Follow High Street to the most northerly point described in the route at the start of this chapter. Instead of doubling left, go straight on, ford a stream in a deep gully, and turn left at the bridleway crossroads just after it. The track drops down to a crossroads (go straight on) before bringing you to Pooley Bridge beside the church. Turn left on the main road.

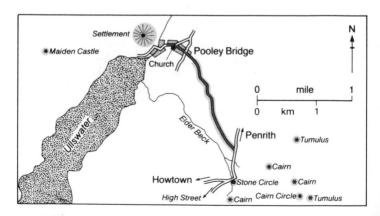

Facilities

PENRITH

A very pleasant market town which has as much to offer as many places within the Lake District national Park but, being a few miles outside it, has not been spoilt. You will find the full range of shops, banks and two cycle shops.

Food and drink

The Agricultural Hotel, Castlegate. Tel. (0768) 62622.

Museum Inn, 17 Castlegate. Tel. (0768) 63576.

Woolpack, Burrowgate. Tel. (0768) 63919.

Accommodation

The Tourist Information Centre at Robinson's School, Middlegate, has an approved list called *Where To Stay In Eden*. It includes all types of accommodation in the area covered in this chapter. Tel. (0768) 67466.

Bike sales and repair

Arragons Cycle Centre, Brunswick Road. Tel. (0768) 890344.

Harpurs Cycles, Middlegate. Tel. (0768) 64475.

Rail travel

Railway Station Tel. (0768) 62466. (London about four hours.)

POOLEY BRIDGE

Shops

General store.

Lake Leisure equipment shop.

Tourist Information

National Park Information Office. Tel. (07684) 86530.

Food, drink and accommodation

The Crown Hotel. Bars, food. Tel. (07684) 86217.

The Swiss Chalet Inn. Bars, food, accommodation. Tel. (07684) 86215 and 86381.

Bikes

Mountain bike hire at Ian Proud Boats. Tel. (07684) 86692.

chapter 3

PATTERDALE to KESWICK

Towns and villages: Keswick, Patterdale and Glenridding
Lakes: Derwent Water and Thirlmere

Introduction to the area

If you were to make just one ride in the Lake District, the ascent of Helvellyn would have to be it. At 3,113 ft (948 m) it is the highest point in England you can legally be on a mountain bike. In terms of height it is just pipped by Scafell Pike and Scafell, but they do not have bridleways to their summits. For the fit and adventurous, this section of the route takes you up and along the Helvellyn range to give several hours of spectacular ridge-top cycling. For the less able, an alternative route runs over gentle ground to the north of the range, following the route of an eighteenth-century coach road.

The only sizeable town in the area is Keswick, a good base for an exploration by mountain bike of northern and western lakeland. It is worth noting that the wilder, more remote and lonely areas such as Wast Water and Ennerdale are much more easily reached from here than they are from southern lakeland.

Even if you plan to avoid peaks and concentrate on low-level cycling, Keswick is still a good place to start mountain biking in the Lakes. From the town there is the relatively easy, hugely rewarding, circuit of Skiddaw. Several excellent pass routes between valleys leave the area wide open to the off-road cyclist. A pass route from the southern tip of Thirlmere over the fells to Watendlath Tarn and down to Borrowdale creates a good, fast link between central and north and western lakeland. I▸

addition, it is possible to link Patterdale with Grasmere on a route running south-west via Grisedale Tarn to Grasmere. (See Chapter 6 for a description.)

Borrowdale, to the south of Derwent Water, is one of the most enchanting dales in the Lake District. There are ancient woodlands over the foothills of the surrounding peaks and along the sheltered banks of the broad River Derwent, and pass routes that offer exciting cycling through to Wastdale and Great Langdale.

The route

From Patterdale to Keswick: 19.5 miles (31.2 km).
Ascent of 710 yds in 4.6 miles (650 m in 7.4 km) from Glenridding to Whiteside Bank. Including Helvellyn detour: 910 yds in 6.5 miles (830 m in 10.4 km).
The ridge route involves a series of swoops from peak to peak. The ascents in each case are as follows:
From Helvellyn to Helvellyn Lower Man: 20 yds over 0.25 miles (18 m over 0.4 km).
From Helvellyn Lower Man to White Side: 65 yds over 0.5 miles (60 m over 0.8 km).
From White Side to Raise: 85 yds over 0.5 miles (78 m over 0.8 km).
From Raise to Stybarrow Dodd: 115 yds over 0.5 miles (105 m over 0.8 km).
From Stybarrow Dodd to Watson's Dodd: negligible ascent.
From Watson's Dodd to Great Dodd: 85 yds over 0.6 miles (78 m over 1 km).
Descent of 700 yds over 5.2 miles (640 m over 8.4 km) from Great Dodd to B5322.
5.8 miles (9.3 km) on metalled roads.
Grade 4.

Cycle north on the A592 to Glenridding. Take the lane on the left just before Glenridding Beck. At the Y-junction take the right fork signposted "Greenside". At the T-junction turn right, crossing the river, and follow the road as it swings left to climb the fell. After a mile (1.6 km), just past the Youth Hostel and

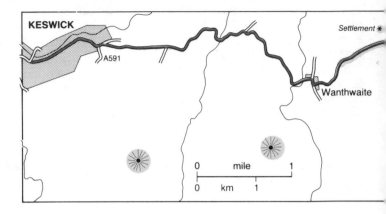

Outdoor Pursuits Centre, the path divides. Do not take the right fork, which climbs to Sticks Pass. Instead, go through a gate beyond the buildings and cross the old lead-mine workings, keeping to the right of Glenridding Beck. When a dam becomes visible look for a path zig-zagging uphill to the right. This half-mile (0.8 km) section is the only part of the ascent that is unrideable. The path levels out and reaches the summit of the Helvellyn range at Whiteside Bank, just to the right (north) of the summit.

If you wish to make a swift, 1.5-mile detour to Helvellyn itself turn left (south) and cross Whiteside Bank for the fairly rough and stony climb to Lower Man. From here you have a fast, smooth ride to the rock steps which lead to Helvellyn's summit.

To continue on the main route turn right at Whiteside Bank (north-east). A third path runs ahead (north-west) and becomes a very steep and dangerous descent to the A591. Not recommended.

Our path climbs gently to the summit of Stybarrow Dodd, then makes a wide curve left to Watson's Dodd. There are fantastic views from here to the north-west over Keswick, Bassenthwaite and Skiddaw, and south-east as far as Windermere. At the 2,600 ft (800 m) mark, half-way towards the top of Great Dodd, the route swings left and becomes a narrow path running in a rut across the fell towards Calfhow Pike.

In fact we swing right before we get to it. No path is visible

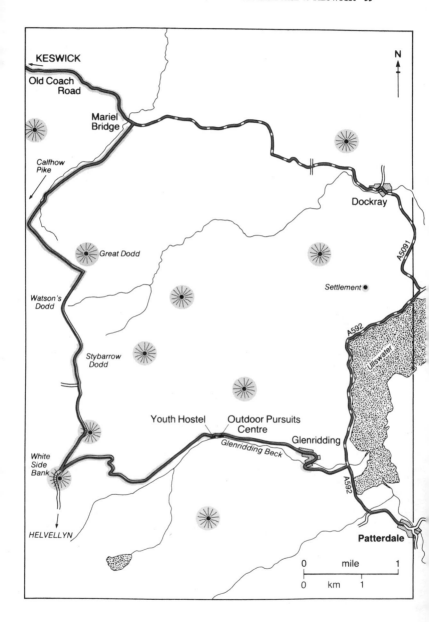

KESWICK

Old Coach
Road

Mariel
Bridge

N

*Calfhow
Pike*

Dockray

A5091

Great Dodd

Settlement ●

*Watson's
Dodd*

A592

Ullswater

*Stybarrow
Dodd*

Youth Hostel

Outdoor Pursuits
Centre

Glenridding

Glenridding Beck

*White
Side
Bank*

A592

HELVELLYN

Patterdale

0		mile		1

| 0 | | km | 1 | |

here, but the route goes off to the right about 200 yds before Calfhow Pike and crosses a stream in a gully just before a wire fence. Follow the fence over very boggy ground and past a sheep-fold for 1.5 miles (2.4 km) to the Old Coach Road which is joined just to the right (east) of Mariel Bridge. The bridge is visible in the last stages of the descent from the fell and is a good marker.

Turn left on the road for a fast descent over loose rocks to the B5322 at Wanthwaite.

Turn right here and then first left on to a lane which swings round to the right before ending at a T-junction after about a mile (1.6 km). Turn left here, then first left and left again. Keep straight on on this lane until it meets the A591. Follow this road into Keswick.

An amended, low-level, version of this route, avoiding the ascent of the Helvellyn range, is covered later in this chapter.

What you will see

On the route: From Helvellyn, there is not much you can't see. The views are stunning. To the north-west are Keswick, Bassenthwaite Lake and the imposing shape of Skiddaw, which may remind you of the Cumberland pencils from junior school days: on the lids of the boxes there used to be a drawing of the mountain – and, seen in the flesh, the fells really do contain all the shades of brown, grey, green and blue that came in the boxes. To the south is a glimpse of Windermere, to the east Ullswater and, hogging the whole horizon, the hog's-back of the High Street range.

Greenside Mine, which you pass on the main route as you leave Glenridding, was once the finest lead mine in the country. From the seventeenth century, when it was first dug, it operated almost continuously until 1962. Excavations reached 3,000 ft (900 m), burrowing beneath the ground for the same distance that Helvellyn soars above it. All that is left now is the spoil, a glum row of miners' cottages, and the pithead buildings, now converted into a Youth Hostel and an Outdoor Pursuits Centre.

In the area: Skiddaw (3,053 ft or 931 m) dominates the town of Keswick and much of the northern lakes.

Derwent Water is rated by many as the best of the lakes. It is 1.25 miles wide, 3 miles long with a maximum depth of 72 ft (2 km by 4.8 km by 22 m). The lake has four islands (plus a fifth made up of floating vegetation which appears every three years or so) and a ferry which stops at several points around the shore. Best views are from Friar's Crag, at the end of the road leading to the lake from Keswick town centre.

Thirlmere is a reservoir, supplying Manchester. Once there were two smaller lakes, Leatheswater and Brackmere, but at the end of the last century the area was dammed and the level raised 51 ft to 160 ft (48 m) at the deepest point. The lake is 0.5 miles wide and 5.5 miles long (0.8 km by 8.8 km). Grisedale Tarn, encountered on the pass route linking Grasmere with Patterdale, is one of the largest and deepest, at over 100 ft (30 m). The setting is spectacular. On a rock by the shore is a memorial commemorating the parting of William Wordsworth and his brother John, who died at sea.

Famous connections

Samuel Taylor Coleridge lived in Keswick, at Greta Hall, now part of Keswick School, from 1800 to 1803. They were miserable years during which his marriage hit the rocks, his health deterioriated and he feared he had lost the ability to write poetry. Not that he disliked the Lakes. In fact he was a dedicated fell walker, one of the first to take to the mountains purely for the pleasure they gave. He often walked from Keswick via Helvellyn to Grasmere, where the Wordsworths lived. Such walks, he said, enriched his imagination and heart. He always took pen, ink and paper in case inspiration came to him on the fells. One night he arrived at Grasmere after a moonlit walk to read part of "Christabel", which he had just composed. He liked his house in Keswick, too, and said of it: "I question if there could be a room in England which commands a view of Mountains and Lakes and Woods and Vales superior to that in which I am now sitting."

Friar's Crag on Derwent Water was a favourite viewpoint of Wordsworth and Coleridge, and of John Ruskin, the great Victorian patron of the arts and social reformer. A memorial to

Ruskin there says "the first thing I remember as an event in life was being taken by Nurse to the brow at Friar's Crag on Derwent Water".

A second memorial at Friar's Crag is to Canon Rawnsley, the one time vicar of Crossthwaite Church, Keswick, who founded the National Trust.

Tennyson is another poet who found inspiration in the area. He was staying at Mirehouse on Bassenthwaite (passed in the Skiddaw circuit later in this chapter) while working on his version of the Arthurian legend. It was while he was walking round the lake that the idea of the throwing of Excalibur into the waters came to him.

The writer Hugh Walpole made Borrowdale, to the south of Derwent Water, his own. He set the four novels in *The Herries Chronicle* there. His story of the Herries family, spanning 200 years, has been compared to John Galsworthy's *Forsyte Saga*. He writes of a Borrowdale in the years before modern transport opened up the remote valleys, of a place enclosed, brooding and suspicious. As one of his characters says of Borrowdale: "Here within these hills, in this space of ground is all the world . . . Lives are lived here completely without any thought of the countries more distant. The mountains close us in." Walpole moved to the area in 1924, living in a house called Brackenburn on the south-west shore of Derwent Water.

Alternative route avoiding ascent of the Helvellyn range: 7 miles (11.3 km).
No notable ascents or descents.
4.5 miles (7 km) on metalled roads.
Grade 1.

Follow the A592 north to its junction with the A5091. Turn left and cycle to Dockray. Turn left on the lane just before the Royal Hotel and follow it until you reach a junction. Go straight on, through a gate on to a track, signposted "Threlkeld". This is the old coach road. Follow it for 5 miles (8 km) until it comes out on the B5322. For the continuation of the route to Keswick refer back to the beginning of this chapter.

Turning the route into a circuit

This is best done by turning right on reaching the old coach road and cycling via Dockray down to the A5091, turning right and picking up the A592. Turn right to return to Glenridding and Patterdale. Grade 1.

Other routes in the area

Circuit from Glenridding via Helvellyn: 5.2 miles (8.4 km).

Ascent of 900 yds in 6.5 miles (830 m in 10.4 km) from Glenridding to Helvellyn.

Descent of 800 yds over 5 miles (730 m over 8 km) from Dollywaggon Pike to Patterdale.

1 mile (1.6 km) on metalled roads.

Grade 4.

In Glenridding, take the lane on the left just before Glenridding Beck. At the Y-junction take the right fork, signposted "Greenside". At the T-junction turn right, crossing the river, and follow the road as it swings left to climb the fell. After a mile (1.6 km), just past the Youth Hostel and Outdoor Pursuits Centre, the path divides. Do not take the right fork, which climbs to Sticks Pass. Instead, go through a gate beyond the buildings and cross the old lead-mine workings, keeping to the right of Glenridding Beck. When a dam becomes visible look for a path zig-zagging uphill to the right. This half-mile (0.8 km) section is the only part of the ascent that is unrideable.

The path levels out and reaches the summit of the Helvellyn range at Whiteside Bank, just to the right (north) of the summit.

Turn left and cross Whiteside Bank for the fairly rough and stony climb to Lower Man. From here you have a fast, smooth ride to the rock steps which lead to Helvellyn's summit. Continue south along the ridge, keeping left when the path divides, to Nethermost Pike. Pass to the right of High Crag and the summit of Dollywaggon Pike before the path swings left and drops to Grisedale Tarn through a series of badly worn zig-zags. You are likely to have to carry the bike here. Turn left at the tarn and look for a path heading downhill in a north-easterly direction, leaving the path around the tarn beside a cairn. There is a rough, rocky descent through Grisedale. As the path begins to level out

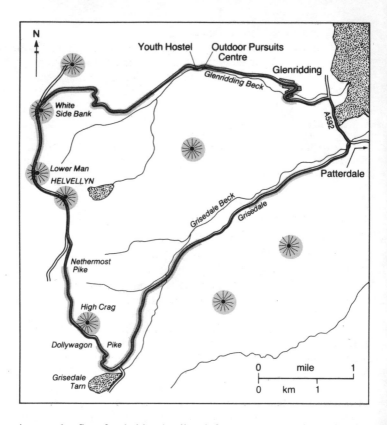

ignore the first footbridge leading left over a stream but take the second. There is now a good swift descent for 2 miles (3 km) until the path joins a lane that comes out on the A592. Turn left to regain your starting-point.

Circuit from Wythburn via Helvellyn: 11.25 miles (18 km).
Ascent of 850 yds over 2.75 miles (780 m over 4.4 km) from Wythburn.
Descent of 800 yds over 2.5 miles (730 m over 4 km) from Sticks Pass.
3.6 miles (5.8 km) on metalled roads.
Grade 5.

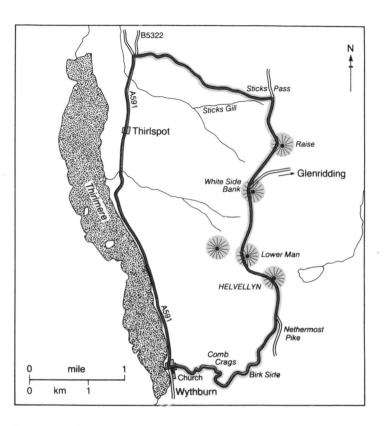

Park at the Wythburn Church car park, on the A591 just at the southern tip of Thirlmere.

The ascent is very steep and the bike must be carried almost all the way. But this painful struggle is well worth it for the spectacular, long-distance ridge route it opens up. The path is very distinct and littered with loose rock. It ascends through a wood and swings round to the right above Comb Crags before swinging left over Birk Side and reaching Nethermost Pike, where it joins the chain of peaks of which Helvellyn is the highest. There are fantastic views over Thirlmere. From here you can actually get on the bike for the half-mile (0.8 km) gentle ascent over gravel to Helvellyn itself.

There are fine views from here through 360 degrees with a particularly impressive view over Ullswater (east) to the great long mass of High Street.

From Helvellyn the route follows the string of summits running north. Leaving the summit in a north-westerly direction aim first for the top of Lower Man, then go north to Whiteside Bank. The descent from Lower Man is steep and rocky and you are likely to have to push for a while. At Whiteside Bank there are three possible routes. To the left a very steep and dangerous descent to the A591 at Thirlspot. Not recommended. To the right a descent to Glenridding. Our route runs north-east over grass to Raise, which has a summit like a rocky moonscape.

The going is now much easier over soft, and sometimes boggy, grass. The path dips to a crossroads at Sticks Pass. Turn left here to begin the descent. The path, over grass, is indistinct at first. Keep Sticks Gill to your left. After a mile the descent steepens markedly and zig-zags, reaching the road at the junction of the A591 and the B5322. Turn left and travel for three miles (4.8 km) back to the starting-point.

Circuit from Keswick around Skiddaw: 18.5 miles (30 km).
Ascent of 100 yds over 2.4 miles (110 m over 3.8 km) from Keswick to car park.
Ascent of 130 yds over 3.6 miles (120 m over 5.8 km) from car park.
11.5 miles (18.4 km) on metalled roads.
Grade 2.

This is an easy, first-rate route.

From Keswick town centre ride up Station Road until it swings left to Briar Rigg. Take the signposted bridleway on the right which climbs up Latrigg to a car park. Go through the gate at the end of the car park and turn immediately left up the narrow path between fences. With the ascent of Skiddaw dead ahead the path divides. Take the less distinct one to the right which crosses White Beck and runs east at 1,150 ft (350 m) on Lonscale Fell.

The path is generally excellent throughout the route, apart from a short rocky section at Lonscale Crags as you round the fell and head north.

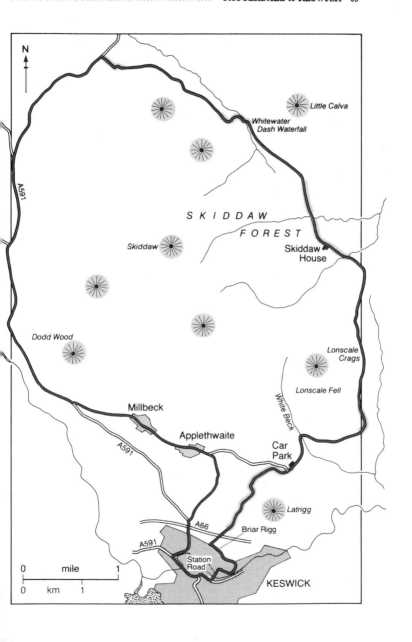

N

Little Calva

Whitewater
Dash Waterfall

S K I D D A W

F O R E S T

Skiddaw

Skiddaw
House

Dodd Wood

Lonscale
Crags

Lonscale Fell

Millbeck

Applethwaite

A591

White Beck

Car
Park

A591

Latrigg

A66

Briar Rigg

A591

Station
Road

KESWICK

0   mile   1

0   km   1

A mile after the crags a bridleway joins from the right, just after you ford a stream. Skiddaw House is now visible, by an isolated clump of trees. Leave the house on the track heading north-west which drops to ford a stream, then climbs Little Calva to the 1,600 ft (480 m) contour and runs to the left, maintaining height before dropping through a hairpin beside Whitewater Dash waterfall and joining a lane. Turn left and, when this lane joins another, left again. At the A591 take another left. Just after Dodd Wood a lane on the left takes you off the main road through Millbeck and Applethwaite before dropping down to the A591 just before its junction with the A66. Go straight on at the roundabout and follow the road back into Keswick.

NB An ascent of Skiddaw is legal, but there is no ridge route or alternative way down. If you want a straight-up, straight-down slog then the route leaves the path described above just after the narrow path between fences which takes you from the car park. The ascent from this point is 640 yds over 3 miles (580 m over 4.8 km). All but the most experienced are likely to have to carry most of the way up and walk most of the way down.
Grade 4.

A linking route from Patterdale to Grasmere is described in Chapter 6.

Linking route from Thirlmere to Borrowdale via Watendlath Tarn: 4 miles (6.4 km).
Ascent of 330 yds over 2.4 miles (300 m over 3.8 km).
Descent of 240 yds over 1.6 miles (220 m over 2.6 km).
Negligible stretch on metalled roads.
Grade 3.

This is a hard ride with a tough, boggy central section. It is enlivened, however, by passing three tarns on its way, and is a quick, efficient way of crossing between these two valleys.
    From the A591 take the lane which runs around the foot of Thirlmere lake. After just under a mile (1.6 km) watch for a sign on the left marked "Bridleway to Watendlath". The path doubles back across a field. At the next gate turn right and climb the rocky ground ahead. The path is indistinct but swings round

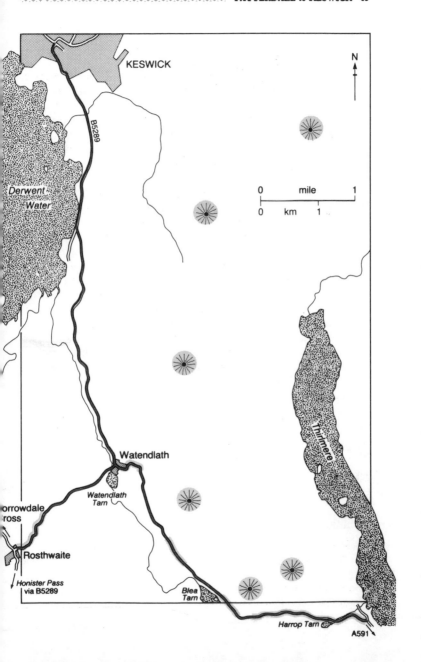

N

KESWICK

B5289

Derwent
Water

0   mile   1
0   km   1

Thirlmere

Watendlath

Watendlath
Tarn

orrowdale
ross

Rosthwaite

Honister Pass
via B5289

Blea
Tarn

Harrop Tarn

A591

to the left to reach a fence over which there is a stile and a gate. Take the gate. You are now in forest, on a path running uphill and emerging shortly at a ford over the outlet stream to Harrop Tarn. Cross the ford to your right and follow the forest track until the first junction. The path to the left is marked "Watendlath footpath" and runs uphill for a few yards to another forest track, on which you turn left.

Watch for a blue bridleway sign pointing up a narrow path to the right. This runs over what looks like a dry river-bed to emerge at a gate on to the open fell. From here the footpath is clear but the bridle path is indistinct. Keep to the left of the footpath, travelling east until you reach the summit. Here there is a fence, breached by two gates. The bridleway gate is the one to the left. Descend from here along the left-hand (northern) shore of Blea Tarn, over boggy grass. At the far end of the tarn a sign points north-north-west up to a cairn on the next summit. Go half-way up the incline before peeling off to the left. You will find a good, grassy descent running down above the gully in which Bleatarn Gill flows. After 0.75 miles (1.2 km) the path becomes distinct and runs to the right of a dry-stone wall. Watendlath Tarn becomes visible to your left. The path goes left and descends over a series of recently reinstated rock zig-zags down to the tarn.

For Keswick turn right and pick up the lane which leads down to the B5289. Follow this north into Keswick.

For Rosthwaite and the foot of Borrowdale cross the bridge and ascend a good, firm path climbing south-west. Where the path forks on the descent go left and you will drop down between stone walls into Rosthwaite village. If you wish to travel further west, turn left on the B5289, which runs over Honister Pass.

NB A linking route from Patterdale to Grasmere is described in Chapter 6.

Facilities

KESWICK
The town has the full range of shops and banks but no cycle shop.
Food and drink
Maysons, Lake Road. Tel. (07687) 74104.

Dog and Gun, Lake Road. Tel. (07687) 73463.
George Hotel, St John's Street, Tel. (07687) 72076.
Accommodation
A very wide range. *Where to Stay* guide from the Tourist Information Centre, Moot Hall, Market Square. Tel. (07687) 72645.

PATTERDALE AND GLENRIDDING
Between them, these two villages, which are less than a mile apart, have reasonable facilities.
Patterdale has a post office selling food and general household goods and a snack bar, and Glenridding has a couple of food shops which cater for walkers and have a good range of packed-lunch foods.
White Lion Inn, Patterdale. Bars, food, accommodation. Tel. (07684) 82214.
Traveller's Rest, Glenridding. Tel. (07684) 82298.
Accommodation
The approved accommodation guide covering this area is called *Where To Stay in Eden*, available from Tourist Information Centres, including Penrith T.I.C., Robinson's School, Middlegate. Tel. (0768) 67466.

chapter 4

KESWICK to ENNERDALE

Towns and villages: Cockermouth, Braithwaite, Loweswater and Buttermere
Lakes: Loweswater, Crummock Water, Buttermere, Ennerdale Water

Introduction to the area

The north-western corner of the Lake District is one of the quietest, gentlest, most relaxing and pleasant of places. Once over the Whinlatter Pass – submerged under the conifer regiments of Thornthwaite Forest – you are in Lorton Vale, where relatively few visitors venture. The three lakes of Loweswater, Crummock Water and Buttermere are on a much smaller scale than anything encountered so far, and inhabit a gentler landscape. There are no famous peaks, either, making this a place of lesser delights. The only villages in this area, Lorton and Buttermere, are very small and well off the main tourist route from Windermere to Keswick. For the first 10 miles (16 km) of this section the cycling is easy and on metalled roads, a respite from the demanding conditions that come both before and after. But once you have cycled over into truly remote Ennerdale you return once more to the sort of rugged, lonely country experienced in earlier chapters.

The area offers three short, self-contained routes, two around lakes and one through forest, that are ideal for the beginner.

The route

From Keswick to Ennerdale: 20 miles (32 km).
Ascent of 215 yds over 2.6 miles (195 m over 4.2 km) from Braithwaite to Thornthwaite.
Descent of 230 yds over 4.4 miles (210 m over 7 km) from Thornthwaite to B5289.
Ascent of 210 yds over 1.8 miles (190 m over 2.9 km) from Loweswater Fell to Floutern Cop.
Descent of 340 yds over 3 miles (310 m over 4.9 km) from Floutern to Ennerdale Water.
10 miles (16 km) on metalled roads.
Grade 3.

From Keswick take the A66 west, towards Cockermouth. Turn left at Braithwaite and follow the B5292 through the village and over Whinlatter Pass towards Lorton Vale. Shortly after you begin to descend take a lane on the left signposted "Hopebeck narrow gated road". (For alternative routes which take you off the road for part of the ride through Whinlatter, see the Thornthwaite Forest section later in this chapter.)

When you reach a T-junction, turn left and the lane emerges on the B5289. Turn left and, at the T-junction a few hundred yards on, take the right fork to Loweswater.

Take the left turn in the hamlet, which leads down past the church and passes the front of the Kirkstile Inn before becoming a track which leads past Kirkstile Farm and through a gate on to the open fell.

Turn right here and follow the track between Mellbreck (on your left) and Loweswater Fell (right). Keep to the main track as it moves to the right into Mosedale, with Gale Fell blocking the way ahead. The track becomes less distinct as it climbs Hen Comb. When it disappears altogether ride diagonally uphill and you will pick up a narrow track which brings you round to the west. At the fence go through the gate. Shortly afterwards the path crosses the fence to your right (north) and runs straight uphill with Floutern Tarn about 200 yds to the left (south).

Shortly after the tarn you begin a steady descent on a distinct, rutted farm track, soon enclosed by stone walls. When your descent to the lane is almost over, the path forks. Go left to

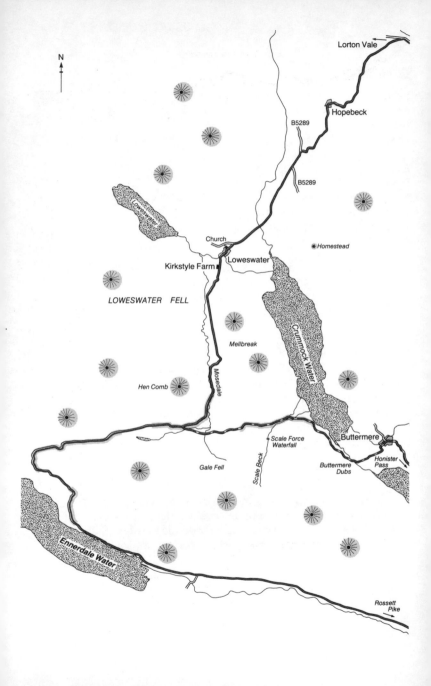

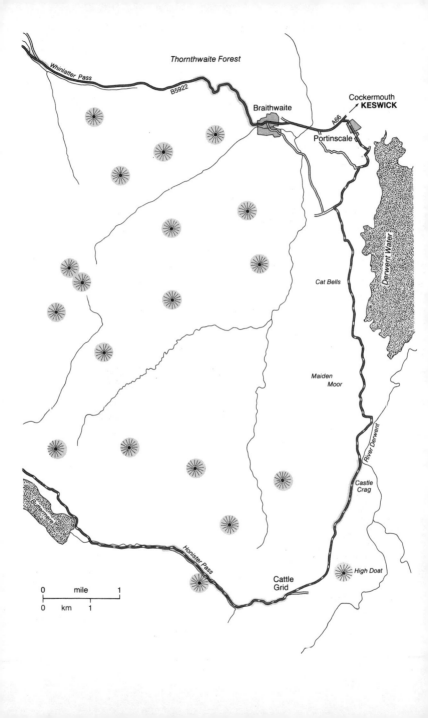

emerge shortly at a lane. Turn left and reach the shores of Ennerdale Water after 1 mile (1.6 km). The route continues as a forest track along the lake's north shore.

What you will see

On the route: Thornthwaite Forest smothers the fells from Braithwaite right across to the Vale of Lorton, but the image-conscious Forestry Commission has made substantial efforts to open the place up to visitors, offering nature trails and picnic sites and hiring out mountain bikes. It is even sold as part of your heritage, being billed as the oldest national forest in the country; it was instituted in 1919 to "create a reserve of timber to meet the nation's need and to provide much-needed jobs". Oh well, that's all right then. There is a visitor centre close to the road which sells maps and gives advice on where to cycle.

Ennerdale, the most westerly of the lakes, is the only one without a road, though a forestry track (which our route uses) runs along the north shore.

In the area: Of all the sixteen lakes, Loweswater is the smallest, prettiest and most easily overlooked. A lane runs along the northern shore but, to the south there is just a bridleway running through the woods that reach down to the shoreline from Loweswater Fell. The lake is 60 ft (18.3 m) deep and measures 1.25 by 0.3 miles (2 km by 0.48 km). Crummock Water and Buttermere, separated merely by a band of low-lying farmland, fill the southern end of the valley as it funnels down towards Honister Pass, the route across into Borrowdale. Crummock Water, the more northerly of the two, is the quieter but lacks a bridleway. It measures 2.5 by 0.5 miles (4 km by 0.8 km) and is up to 144 ft (43 m) deep. Buttermere, which can be cycled around, is 1.25 by 0.3 miles (2 km by 0.48 km) and 80 ft (24 m) deep.

Famous connections

The Fish Inn at Buttermere was the home of Mary Robinson, who became famous as the Maid of Buttermere, a woman wronged. The story of how the innkeeper's beautiful daughter was duped by a confidence trickster has been told for centuries, most recently in a novel by Melvyn Bragg, FC (Famous Cumbrian). In the eighteenth century it was a scandal that enraged the nation, including Wordsworth and Coleridge. A character calling himself the Hon. Augustus Hope arrived in Keswick, spent freely and mixed with smart society. He charmed and married the maid, only to be revealed as a swindler with wives and children all over the country, and no money whatsoever. He was hanged.

Wordsworth was so outraged that he mentions the episode in *The Prelude* where he says "unfaithful to a virtuous wife, deserted and deceived, the spoiler came and wooed the artless daughter of the hills, and wedded her, in cruel mockery." She and the inn became quite a tourist attraction.

Hugh Walpole, author of *The Herries Chronicle*, loved Cat Bells, the gentle peak to the west of Derwentwater. Walpole moved to the Lakes in 1924, buying a house called Brackenburn on the lower slopes of the mountain. He died there in 1941 and is buried in St John's Churchyard, Keswick.

Ennerdale is the scene of Wordsworth's poem "The Brothers", which is based on the story of a shepherd boy who died on Pillar Rock, "the loneliest place of all these hills", which can be seen towering to the south. The boy's brother, who has been at sea for years, returns and is told the story of the death by the priest. He points out the fatal place thus:

"You see yon precipice – it almost looks
Like some vast building made of many crags
And in the midst is one particular rock
That rises like a column from the vale."
It was from here the boy fell.
". . . in his hands he must have had
His Shepherd's staff; for midway in the cliff
It had been caught, and there for many years
It hung – and moulder'd there."

Ennerdale was one of Coleridge's favourite lakes, but the afforestation means that neither poet would recognise the place today.

Turning the main route into a circuit
From Mosedale to Braithwaite: 17 miles.
Descent of 120 yds over 2.4 miles (110 m over 3.9 km) from Mosedale to Buttermere Dubs.
Ascent of 240 yds over 2.8 miles (220 m over 4.5 km) up Honister Pass.
Descent of 260 yds over 3.2 miles (240 m over 5.1 km) from top of Honister Pass to River Derwent.
11 miles (17.6 km) on metalled roads.
Grade 2.

To turn this section of the route into a circuit involves navigating one very boggy section and then a tough road climb over Honister Pass, but the reward is a truly first-rate run north along the western shore of Derwent Water on bridle track and lane. We think the latter makes the former worth it, but you may not agree!

The return route leaves the path described at the start of the climb from Mosedale. Instead of climbing to the west, cut straight on to the foot of Gale Fell and turn left (east) to descend over very wet and boggy ground which crosses Scale Beck below Scale Force waterfall and runs south-east along the shore of Crummock Water. Take the bridge to your left over Buttermere Dubs (the river running between the two lakes) and follow the track into Buttermere village. Turn left (south) on the lane and follow it over Honister Pass. Half a mile (0.8 km) down the other side, watch for a flinty track, marked "Bridleway", leaving the lane at a narrow angle to the left just before a cattle grid. After half a mile (0.8 km) the track becomes harder to follow. Ignore clear paths going downhill, but proceed just to the east of north, climbing over grass and keeping High Doat to your right. From here the cycling is fantastic: a fast run on a smooth path, then a rocky but very rideable descent through the old quarry below Castle Crag before emerging on the shore of the River Derwent. Keep on the left bank and take the lower of two lanes leaving the woods. At Grange turn left onto a lane running north. The route runs between Maiden Moor and Cat Bells to your left and Derwent Water to your right. At a junction go as near to straight on as you can. Once through the village of Portinscale you emerge on the A66. Turn left for Braithwaite.

Other routes in the area

Thornthwaite Forest circuit: 7 miles (11.2 km).
Ascent of 120 yds over 1 mile (110 m over 1.6 km) from Visitor Centre to Horsebox Crossroads.
Descent of 170 yds over 3 miles (155 m over 4.8 km) from Horsebox Crossroads to B5292.
Ascent of 50 yds over 2.6 miles (45 m over 4.1 km) from junction with B5292 back to Visitor Centre.
1 mile (1.6 km) on metalled roads.
Grade 3.

NB If you are cycling through Whinlatter Pass on the route covered earlier and want a diversion, the first section of this ride, until it regains the B5292, will get you off the road, but will increase your journey time by an hour.

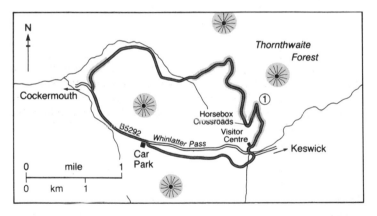

The Forestry Commission allows cycling throughout the forest but recommends, and has waymarked with white arrows on a green background, the following route among others.

Climb the track behind the Visitor Centre north to location post No 1. The path then doubles back south to Horsebox Crossroads. Turn left as you emerge on the wide track here and follow it as it swings right and climbs. You soon begin a fast, smooth descent on a wide forest track which sweeps in a rough arc to the left to emerge after three miles (4.8 km) at the B5292.

Turn left and ride up the road for a mile (1.6 km) before taking a track which leaves the car park to the right. Follow it east, parallel with the road, until you reach a junction. Turn left, downhill, for the B5292. Turn left for the Visitor Centre, which is a few hundred yards away to the right of the road.

Loweswater lake circuit: 5 miles (8 km).
No major ascents or descents.
2 miles (3 km) on metalled roads.
Grade 1.

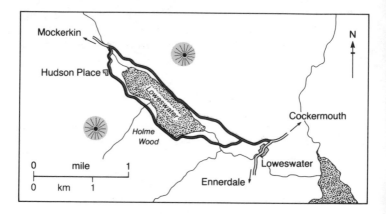

From Loweswater village take the lane running north-west. Look for a turning to the left at the summit of the hill coming out of the village, marked "Public Bridleway". The lane runs across fields and becomes a track running through woods on the southern shore of the lake. Follow the track beyond the lake to climb to Hudson Place. Turn right to reach the lane running to the north of the lake. Turn right here to regain your starting-point.

Buttermere lake circuit: 5.2 miles (8.3 km).
No major ascents or descents.
2.2 miles (3.5 km) on metalled roads.
Grade 1.

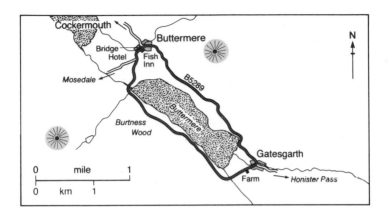

Turn down between the Bridge Hotel and Fish Inn and take the bridleway. Where it forks go left to cross the stream at the top of Buttermere and climb through woods on the other side. Take the higher of the two paths for a smooth, easy ride to the foot of the lake. Turn left, and the path passes Gatesgarth Farm to emerge at the B5289. Turn left to regain your starting-point.

Facilities

COCKERMOUTH
A charming small town with a pleasant, broad main street offering good basic facilities away from the tourist traps of the National Park.

Food and drink
Quince and Medlar, Castlegate. One of the best vegetarian restaurants in the country. Tel. (0900) 823579.
Old Court House Restaurant, Main Street. Tel. (0900) 823871.
Courtyard Coffee House, Headford Crescent, Main Street. Tel. (0900) 823971.
Brown Cow, Main Street. Tel. (0900) 823174.
Swan Inn, Kirkgate. Tel. (0900) 822425.
Cheers, Main Street. Tel. (0900) 822109.
The Pheasant Inn, Bassenthwaite Lake. Tel. (059681) 234.

Accommodation
Approved list from the Tourist Information Centre, Riverside
Car Park, Market Street. Tel. (0900) 822634.
Youth Hostel, Double Mills, Cockermouth. Tel. (0900) 822561.

BRAITHWAITE
There is a well-stocked general store and Book Cottage, which
combines as a cafe and second-hand bookshop.
Food, drink, accommodation
Royal Oak Inn. Bars, food and restaurant. Tel. (059682) 533.
Coledale Inn. Bar, food and accommodation. Tel. (059682) 272.
Ivy House Hotel. Accommodation, restaurant. Tel. (059682)
338.
Bikes
The general store also hires mountain bikes and sells spares. Tel.
(059682) 273.

LORTON
Post Office sells food.
Pub
Wheatsheaf Inn, Low Lorton. Tel. (090085) 268.

LOWESWATER
The Kirkstile Inn. Bar, food, accommodation. Tel. (090085) 219.

BUTTERMERE
Croft Farm snack bar.
The Bridge Hotel. Bar, food, accommodation. Tel. (059685) 252
or 266.
The Fish Inn. Bar, food, accommodation. Tel. (059685) 253.
Youth Hostel: King George VI Memorial Hostel. Tel. (059685)
245.

ENNERDALE
Youth Hostel: Cat Crag. Tel. (0946) 861237.

THORNTHWAITE FOREST
Whinlatter Visitor Centre, open daily, sells maps of the forest,
drinks and souvenirs, and hires mountain bikes. Tel. (059682)
469.

chapter 5

ENNERDALE to ROSSETT PIKE

Villages: Wasdale Head, Eskdale Green, Boot
Lakes: Wast Water

Introduction to the area

The 12 miles (19.3 km) of this short section of the route pack in a great deal of pure, unadulterated mountain cycling. If you have been following the main route from its start in Windermere, this is what you have been preparing for.

The route is remote, rugged, demanding and hugely rewarding. After the tough climb over Black Sail Pass from Ennerdale to Wasdale the comforts of the Wasdale Head Inn will provide a welcome break – and allow you to stock up on food, drink and other essential resources before the trek across into Langdale.

There are linking routes here with Borrowdale and from Wastdale to Eskdale. There is also an alternative route between Ennerdale and Wasdale.

It is not practical to turn this route into a circuit.

The route

12 miles (19.3 km) from Ennerdale to Rosset Pike.
Ascent of 385 yds over 1.2 miles (350 m over 1.9 km) from Ennerdale to Black Sail Pass.
Descent of 500 yds over 2.4 miles (460 m over 3.85 km) from Black Sail Pass to Wastdale Head.
Ascent of 500 yds over 2.4 miles (460 m over 1.5 km) from

Wasdale Head to Sty Head Tarn.
Descent of 438 yds over 2 miles (400 m over 3.2 km) from Angle
Tarn to Mickleden.
No metalled roads.
Grade 4.

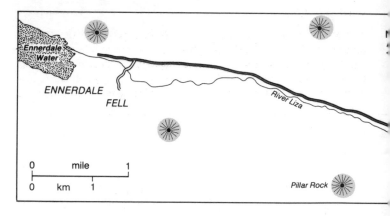

From the head of Ennerdale Water follow the forestry track as
it runs gently uphill. After four miles (6.4 km) you will come to
Black Sail Youth Hostel. In front of it, the path swings right,
crosses the River Liza and begins the ascent to Black Sail Pass.
The ascent is clear but rocky and to the left of the stream.

Bikes must be carried, as they must for the first leg of the
descent into Mosedale. The path runs to the left of Mosedale
Beck and becomes a track running between stone walls as it
approaches the back of the Wasdale Head Inn.

Cross Frogmire Beck by the bridge and turn left if you wish to
continue cycling; but go straight on, alongside Mosedale Beck,
for the hotel.

From Wasdale Head the path follows a long steady ascent up
the old pack-pony route called Moses Trod. The way is rocky
but rideable for about 1.5 miles (2.4 km). After one mile
(1.6 km), where the path splits, follow the left hand route, which
runs up the fellside away from the stream.

At Sty Head go straight on, keeping Sty Head Tarn away to

your left. There is a rocky climb and descent before Sprinkling Tarn. Once again, keep the tarn on your left and go straight on. Ascend Allen Crags before dropping to Angle Tarn. Continue the descent towards Mickleden and Langdale.

What you will see

The area around Wasdale is one of the holy places of the British mountain climbing fraternity, because it was here that British climbing began in the last century. Famous peaks like Great Gable, Scafell and Scafell Pike, at 3,200 ft (977 m) the highest mountain in England, provided the first great challenges to

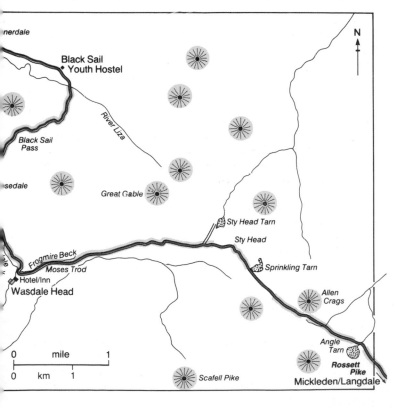

British climbers. The notorious Pillar Rock is another of the famous names from the early days of climbing.

The Wasdale Head Inn is something of a shrine for mountaineers. The old photographs and the collection of climbing equipment hung up around Ritson's Bar testify to its rich and fascinating history. Ritson's Bar is named after Will Ritson: he was one of the great Cumbrian characters, the first landlord of the pub, who was granted a licence in 1856 and died in 1890.

Ritson claimed to have been a friend of Wordsworth and De Quincey. He also claimed to have been the biggest liar in England – a competition is held at the Santon Bridge Inn every four years in his memory (politicians and journalists are not allowed to enter, presumably because they are considered to be professional liars!).

Wasdale is a place rich in climbing folklore and redolent with other mythology. The path Moses Trod, for example, is said to mark the route taken by a man called Moses, a famous smuggler, although there seems to be some debate about what exactly he smuggled. One theory is that he traded in plumbago. Keswick and its pencil industry built a fortune from plumbago which used to be mined in Borrowdale. According to Wainwright, Moses was a Honister quarryman who illegally made whiskey from bog-water.

It is one of the most dramatic landscapes in Britain, literally the high point of the Lake District. The view of Great Gable seen from the southern end of Wast Water is so symbolic of the Lake District that the National Park Authority has used this scene for the Lake District National Park logo.

Wasdale's claim to fame is that it has the highest mountain (Scafell Pike), the deepest lake (Wast Water), the smallest church and the biggest liar in England. The last two are open to question, but the highest mountain and deepest lake are certainly true. Wast Water has an average depth of 120 ft (36 m) – and a maximum depth of 260 ft (79 m). Its depth means that, surprisingly, the lake rarely freezes.

Separated from the main part of the Lake District by the hair-raising road that runs along Hardknott and Wrynose Passes, Wasdale is less frequented by tourists and, perhaps more than anywhere in this region, has managed to retain its original character and ambience.

Famous connections

Samuel Taylor Coleridge may not have been able to claim to be the biggest liar in England, he could however, claim credit for the first recorded ascent of Scafell Pike. Coleridge was hardly a model climber: once he reached the top of a mountain, he confessed that he could not be bothered with the boring twists and turns offered by a safe path downhill. He preferred to plunge helter-skelter down the fastest and straightest way.

The account of his descent of Scafell suggests that he was lucky not to have broken his neck. He came down through Broad Stand – probably not the route the Rambler's Association would recommend – and found himself slithering down what turned out to be the precipitous dry course of a waterfall.

My limbs were all in a tremble. I lay upon my back to rest myself, and was beginning according to my custom to laugh at myself for a madman, when the sight of the crags above me on each side, and the impetuous clouds just over them, posting so luridly and so rapidly to northward, overawed me.

Other routes in the area

Circuit of Wast Water: 15.5 miles (24.8 km).
Mostly level ride for 8 miles (12.8 km) on metalled road from Eskdale Green to turn-off before Wasdale Head.
From Wasdale up to Tongue Moor, ascent of 257 yds over 1.25 miles (235 m over 2 km); similar rate of descent back to Eskdale Green.
Grade 3.

For this tour we start in Eskdale Green, which probably makes the most practical starting- and finishing-point. In the centre of the village, near the Outward Bound Mountain School, there is a small car park, public toilets and phone box. From here follow the road west to Santon Bridge.

At Santon Bridge, before you reach the bridge over the River Irt, turn right and travel down to Wast Water. Here the road follows the western shoreline of the lake, dramatically over-shadowed by The Screes, a sheer mass of rock rearing up on the opposite side of Wast Water.

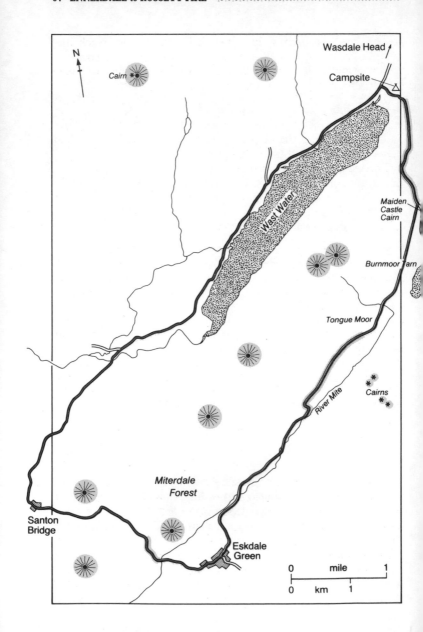

The road is narrow but metalled. When you reach the campsite at the foot of Wasdale Head at the top of the lake, the easiest – and fastest – part of the circuit is over. You will now be carrying your bike for a large part of the rest of the trip.

There are clear signs here for the public bridleway to Eskdale Green. The rocky, unrideable path leads up the side of the hill.

At the top of the hill, at the place marked Maiden Castle Cairn on the map, the path becomes indistinct. Without a compass and a sure grasp of the principles of map-reading, it's easy to get lost here. We did. What was a mild, grey but not unpleasant day was suddenly transformed into the storm scene from King Lear. Rain came down horizontally, threatening to turn the map into papier mâché. A thick mist also descended, obscuring any possible landmarks.

A short way further on, the mist eased to offer a glimpse of Burnmoor Tarn. In order to gain the path for Eskdale, it's important to get the tarn on your near left. Struggling with the bicycle on your shoulder through a boggy, barren landscape – and attempting to find your way at the same time – can be a wholly cheerless experience. It's tempting to sit down and cry: it's probably best not to. Comfort yourself with the thought that this is the sort of thing for which multinational companies pay thousands of pounds to test the character of their senior executives.

If you've guessed right, you should eventually recover the path which shortly leads to what seems to be the top of a cliff. You may wonder whether attempting to descend this semi-precipitous waterfall is the act of a rational human being – particularly with a mountain bike in tow.

Take a tip from Coleridge: don't think twice, it's all right – but take it carefully. At the bottom of the hill you're in a small valley, confronted with yet another awesome landscape of monolithic slabs of rock and barren hills. You follow the stream – the River Mite – almost right back to Eskdale.

At Low Place, the path at last becomes properly rideable once more. Follow the sign to Eskdale Green through the farmyard. There is a short cut back to the village from a point along this track, but it's probably best to stay on the main track until you reach the road at Eskdale Green. Turn left, and continue straight on until you return to the car park.

Linking route from Wasdale Head to Boot: 5.25 miles (8.4 km).
The first mile (1.6 km) to camp site at head of Wast Water on
metalled road. From camp site to Maiden Castle Cairn, ascent
of 246 yds over 1.5 miles (225 m over 2.4 km).
From Maiden Castle Cairn to Boot a descent of 257 yds over 3.75
miles (235 m over 6 km).
Grade 3.

Follow the above route until the point near Maiden Castle Cairn.
Instead of branching right for Miterdale and Eskdale Green,
keep left towards Burnmoor Tarn. Cross the bridge and proceed

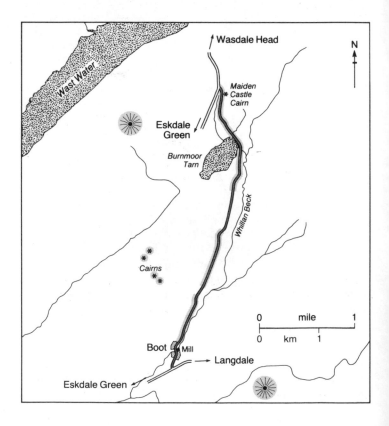

along the path which runs above Whillan Beck (don't actually go down to the stream), and continue down to Boot, emerging at the old mill.

Linking route from Sty Head to Seathwaite and Borrowdale: 2 miles (3.2 km).
Descent of 410 yds over 2 miles (375 m over 3.2 km).
No distance on metalled roads.
Grade 3.

The route from Sty Head down to Seathwaite is straight, direct and relatively easy to follow. The path leads down to the left of Styhead Tarn before following Styhead Gill round to Greenhow Knott and Stockley Bridge and then dropping to Seathwaite.

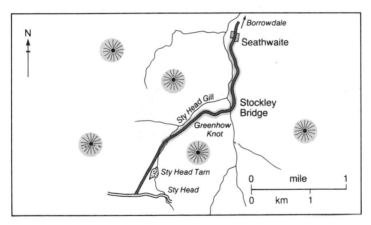

Linking route from Wasdale to Ennerdale: 8 miles (12.8 km).
Ascent of 580 yds over 5.25 miles (530 m over 8.4 km).
Descent of 540 yds over 2.75 miles (494 m over 4.4 km).
No metalled roads.
Grade 4.

The first problem is finding the start of the bridle path off the road that runs along Wast Water. The landmark to look for is Nether Beck, which runs into the lake at Nether Beck Bridge two

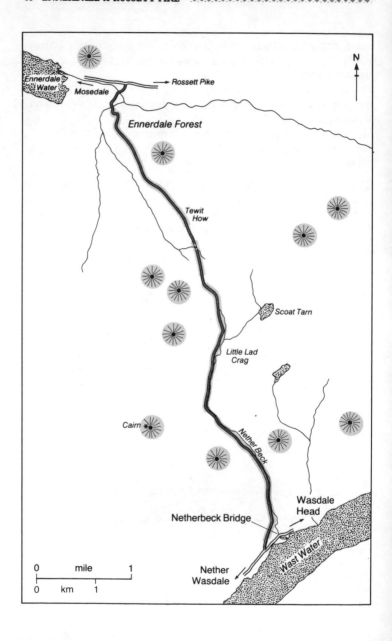

N

Ennerdale
Water

Mosedale

Rossett Pike

Ennerdale Forest

Tewit
How

Scoat Tarn

Little Lad
Crag

Cairn

Nether Beck

Wasdale
Head

Netherbeck Bridge

Nether
Wasdale

Wast Water

0   mile   1

0   km   1

and a half miles (4 km) from the Wasdale Head Inn. Lug your bike up the steep path which follows Nether Beck on its western side.

Near Little Lad Crag, the path of the stream heads north-east to Scoat Tarn: make the steep climb north over the ridge, descending towards Tewit How where the track descends rapidly to Ennerdale Forest; here the path becomes rideable once more. Follow the path round as it skirts the northern end of Ennerdale Water.

Facilities

WASDALE HEAD

The Wasdale Head Inn, Tel. (09406) 229, serves food and offers accommodation. There is also a shop beside the pub, selling general outdoor clothing and equipment.

Near the lake is a National Trust campsite.

BOOT

A charming Lakeland hamlet with a sub-post office selling food, a corn mill and three pubs: the Burnmoor Inn, Tel. (09403) 224, the Woolpack Inn, Tel. (09403) 230 and the Brook House Hotel, Tel. (09403) 288. This is the Eskdale terminus of the Ravenglass & Eskdale Railway (see below): the station has its own café and shop.

ESKDALE GREEN

The home of the Outward Bound Mountain School, it has some shops – including an outdoor equipment shop – and several good pubs, including: King George IV, Tel. (09403) 262 and Bower House Inn, Tel. (09403) 262. It also has a National Westminster Bank open for four hours on Tuesdays!

THE RAVENGLASS & ESKDALE RAILWAY

England's oldest narrow gauge steam railway, known locally as "T'laal Ratty", has been operating between Ravenglass on the coast and Eskdale for more than 100 years. Trains run daily from the beginning of April to the end of October – there is a reduced service off-season.

The train will carry bicycles subject to space being available on an open coach. The Ratty's services connect with British Rail's Cumbrian Coast services between Carlisle, Barrow-in-Furness and Lancaster. If you're travelling to the Lake District without a car, the Ratty provides a good way of quickly getting into the heart of some of the Lake District's best mountain biking country.

A one-way ticket from Ravenglass to Eskdale (Dalegarth) costs £2.40 (bikes are carried free of charge); the seven-mile journey takes 40 minutes. For further information contact: The Ravenglass & Eskdale Railway Co. Ltd, Ravenglass, Cumbria CA18 1SW, Tel. (0229) 717171. Information on local British Rail services is available from the booking office at Carlisle Station Tel. (0228) 44711.

chapter 6

ROSSETT PIKE to LITTLE LANGDALE

Towns and villages: Ambleside and Grasmere
Lakes: Rydal Water, Grasmere and Elterwater

Introduction to the area

Our Lake District mountain bike circular route cuts through only a small corner of this section – you should make time to branch off on the other suggested routes to see as much as you can of this region.

The route itself follows the Cumbrian Way along a valley that runs between the Langdale Pikes and Bow Fell. Although it's only a short drive away to busy Lake District places such as Ambleside, there are plenty of walkers and mountain bikers but few common-or-garden tourists.

The one diversion you must make is to Grasmere, with its strong Wordsworth links, arguably the most beautiful and the most attractively located of all Lakeland towns. Using your bike to explore Grasmere and neighbouring Ambleside you will quickly discover the benefits of travelling on two wheels rather than four. At busy times, the car parks fill up and the roads get clogged with traffic.

Within a few minutes of leaving Dove Cottage, for example, while motorists are still trying to get out of the car park you can be heading up a mountain track with only sheep for company.

There are linking routes in this section to Stonethwaite and Borrowdale.

The route

3 miles (4.8 km), from Mickleden to Little Langdale.
Ascent of 245 yds over 1 mile (224 m over 1.6 km).
Descent of 103 yds over 1.8 miles (94 m over 2.9 km).
2 miles (3.2 km) on metalled roads.
Grade 4.

The path descends, with Rossett Gill on the right, into Mickleden. A footbridge takes you across Mickleden Beck, after which a broad path runs along the valley floor with the beck to the right.

At Middle Fell farm turn right to drop down past the Dungeon

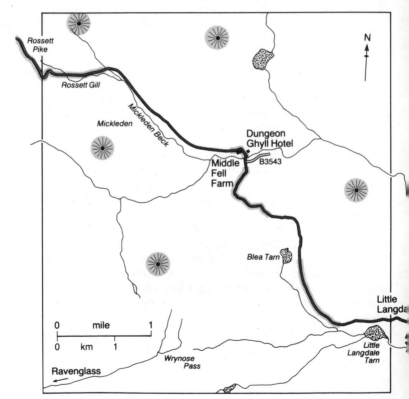

Ghyll Hotel to the B5343. Turn right on the road, which almost immediately bends left to climb steeply past Blea Tarn and over into Little Langdale. Soon after passing Little Langdale Tarn to your right look out for a narrow lane on the right.

What you will see

Wordsworth said of Langdale that it "should on no account be missed by him who has a true enjoyment of grand separate Forms composing a sublime Unity, austere but reconciled and rendered attractive to the affections by the deep serenity that is spread over everything".

The epic nature of the scenery is the key attraction. Wordsworth, who knew a thing or two about the best Lake District places, considered this area a favourite spot.

He was particularly fond of Dungeon Ghyll Force waterfalls:

"Into a chasm a mighty block
Hath fallen, and made a bridge of rock:
The gulf is deep below;
And in a basin black and small,
Receives a lofty waterfall."

The Wrynose pass which runs west from Little Langdale follows the course of the old Roman road from Ambleside to Ravenglass.

Famous connections

For mountain bikers travelling with a copy of *The Prelude* nestling beside their puncture repair kit, this area will provide the literary highpoint of their ride.

Grasmere is a town synonymous with the poet William Wordsworth. He came here to live in 1799 when he was 29, and stayed in the town until 1813, when he moved to Rydal Mount a few miles south.

The Grasmere house most closely associated with the poet is Dove Cottage, in which he lived from 1799 to 1808. A neighbouring barn has been converted into a fascinating museum, which excellently presents the story of Wordsworth's life and his poetry. The museum contains a wide variety of

Wordsworth's possessions and keepsakes, from his ice skates and sandwich box to a lock of the poet's hair.

The short tour of Dove Cottage provides an intriguing insight into the simple, unsophisticated life of the Wordsworths during their residence in what must have been a very overcrowded house. When the list of residents included Wordsworth, his wife, his sister, his sister-in-law, his children and finally Thomas De Quincey, who took over the tenancy, the poet decided that they needed a place with more room.

Wordsworth's friendship with De Quincey, the author of *Confessions of an English Opium Eater*, came to an abrupt end when he knocked down the Wordsworths' much-loved summer-house after he took possession of Dove Cottage.

Sir Walter Scott visited the Wordsworths at Dove Cottage, but he is believed to have found their plain living a little too ascetic for his taste. On one morning he is said to have climbed out of his bedroom window to take a large breakfast at The Swan Inn before sneaking back to his room at Dove Cottage.

From Dove Cottage, the Wordsworths moved to Allan Bank, where the family enjoyed the luxury of each having a room to themselves. Wordsworth received permission to plant forest trees in the park, some of which can still be seen. From Allan Bank, in 1811, the family moved to the Old Vicarage, where they lived for two years. Neither Allan Bank nor the Old Vicarage are open to the public.

The Wordsworths' final home was Rydal Mount, two miles south of Grasmere, where the poet lived until his death in 1850. Rydal Mount, like Dove Cottage, is owned by the Wordsworth Trust and is open to the public. The family's move to Rydal coincided with Wordsworth's becoming Official Distributor of Stamps for Westmorland, which earned him the princely sum of £300 a year, enough to guarantee the family a comfortable life. Wordsworth became Poet Laureate in 1843 after the death of fellow lakeland poet Southey.

Wordsworth is buried in St Oswald's Church in Grasmere, along with his wife Mary, sister Dorothy, sister-in-law Sara, and his children Catherine and Thomas, who died in childhood. Nearby is the grave of Coleridge's eldest son Hartley, Wordsworth's godson.

Other routes in the area

Circuit from Ambleside via Grasmere Lake and Rydal Water: 6.8 miles (11 km).

Ascent of 110 yds over 0.8 miles (100 m over 1.3 km) from lane to Miller Brow.
Descent of 98 yds over 1.4 miles (90 m over 2.25 km) from Red Bank to Rydal Water.
2 miles (3.2 km) on metalled roads.
Grade 2.

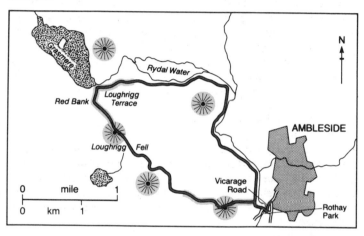

Leave Ambleside on the road, Millans Park, that leads off Compston Road alongside Zeffirelli's restaurant and cinema. Turn immediately left on to Vicarage Road, ending at Rothay Park.

Walk across the park, over a bridge to a lane. Turn right in the lane and almost immediately left up a steep lane. There is a sign for Loughrigg, and the whole route is well waymarked. When the lane ends the route continues over grass, keeping close to a wall on the right.

There are views left (south) to Windermere and ahead (west) to Elterwater. Keep to the main path curving round the fell to the right, ignoring a clear path running downhill to the left beneath Ivy Crag.

The route joins a lane, and there are signs for a caravan site on the right. Go straight ahead and right on to the main lane leading towards Grasmere. Follow it to Red Bank, just before a steep descent. A gate to the right (marked "footpath", though it is in fact a bridleway) takes you on a wide track across Loughrigg terrace – a fine, smooth, gentle descent.

Grasmere and then Rydal Water are clearly visible below on the left (north). Where the paths split, take the lower one, which descends to Rydal Water's shore before climbing up to a track ending in a lane. Turn right to complete the circle.

Pass route from Grasmere to Patterdale via Grisedale Tarn: 6.6 miles (10.6 km).
Ascent of 495 yds over 2.4 miles (450 m over 3.8 km) from the main road to Grisedale Tarn.
Descent of 460 yds over 4.2 miles (420 m over 6.7 km) from Grisedale Tarn to Patterdale.
Negligible distance on metalled roads.
Grade 4.

A thoroughly enjoyable, very largely rideable route. The path leaves the A591, travelling north-west on the bridleway at Mill Bridge, just north of the Travellers' Rest.

It climbs up a well-surfaced track to emerge on the fells at a ford. Take the path to the left, which climbs smoothly over grass before swinging right and levelling out. All this is rideable, and there are fine views back to Grasmere lake.

The path then swings left and climbs (unrideably) over loose rock for two or three hundred yards before emerging on the plateau at Grisedale Tarn. The path runs around to the north-eastern corner of the tarn, where the water escapes out into Grisedale Beck.

The zig-zag path to the north leads up to the summit of Dollywaggon Pike. Turn right at the cairn beside the stream to begin the descent, over loose rock, to Patterdale. The path is unrideable for a few hundred yards, but then levels out as it approaches the valley floor. Cross the stream by the second bridge and follow the path down to the lane, which leads out to the A592. Turn right for Patterdale village, right for Glenridding.

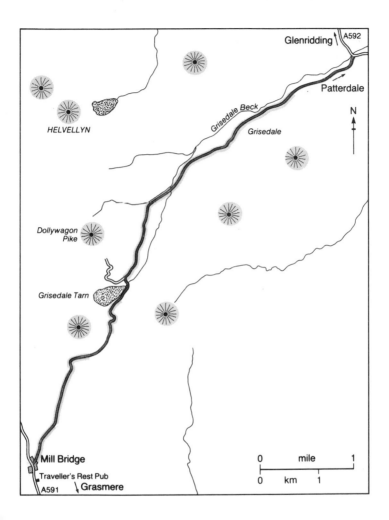

Pass route from Langdale to Borrowdale via Stake Pass: 7.5 miles (12.2 km).

Ascent of 370 yds over 3.6 miles (340 m over 5.8 km) from Great Langdale to Stake Pass.

Descent of 306 yds over 2.4 miles (280 m over 3.8 km) from

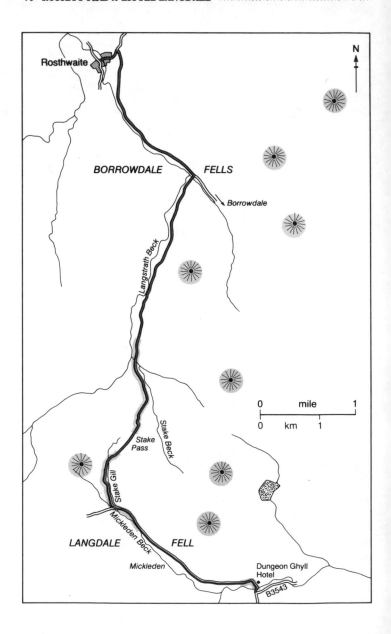

Rosthwaite

BORROWDALE   FELLS

Borrowdale

Langstrath Beck

N

0   mile   1

0   km   1

Stake Beck

Stake
Pass

Stake Gill

Mickleden Beck

LANGDALE   FELL

Mickleden

Dungeon Ghyll
Hotel

B3543

Stake Pass to Langstrath.
Negligible distance on metalled road.
Grade 5.

From the end of the B5343 in Langdale turn right and cycle round the back of the Dungeon Ghyll Hotel, where you pick up a bridleway signposted "Mickleden". A good, wide path runs along the valley floor, with Mickleden Beck to the left.

After 2 miles (3.6 km) and just past a footbridge, Stake Pass is signposted off to the right. The route climbs steeply, following a series of zig-zags, with Stake Gill to the right. At the summit is an unusual plateau, which continues for several hundred yards before the path begins a steep, rocky descent into Borrowdale.

This is the toughest part of the route. Once across Stake Beck via a footpath things begin to level out, but the going is still rocky. The path continues, with Langstrath Beck to the left, to a gate which leads onto an area of flat rock. Going straight across it, pick up a footbridge which leads to a T-junction.

Turn left for the descent to Rosthwaite. The path is soon enclosed by stone walls. When you hit a tarmacked drive turn left over a hump-backed bridge to the road. Turn left for Rosthwaite, right to travel north up Borrowdale.

Pass route from Grasmere to Borrowdale: 7.5 miles (12 km).
From Grasmere to Ferngill Crag, ascent of 477 yds over 3.25 miles (436 m over 5.2 km).
Short descent, then climb to Greenup Edge of 80 yds over 0.75 miles (73 m over 1.2 km).
Descent of 577 yds over 3.5 miles (528 m over 5.6 km).
Very small distance on metalled road.
Grade 4.

Leave Grasmere by the Easedale Road, following signs for Easedale Tarn. After half a mile (0.8 km), the path to Easedale Tarn is signposted to the left over a small footbridge. Ignore this sign and continue straight on towards Brimmer Head Farm, where on your right begins the footpath up towards Ferngill Crag.

The early part of the path is flat but because of the condition

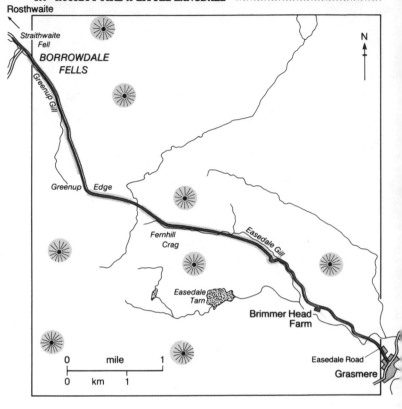

of the track it is mostly unrideable. As you get nearer Ferngill Crag, the path becomes very steep – pulling the bicycle up becomes hard work. From Ferngill Crag the path descends slightly – allowing you the brief luxury of getting on your bike – before sharply rising again to Greenup Edge.

The path levels out across a short plateau before a fairly terrifying precipitous descent towards Stonethwaite Fell. The climb down this sheer drop is made more hazardous by the loose stones that slide away under your feet, threatening to pitch you head over heels with the bike down the steep slope.

As you descend, the path begins to level out, but it is never good enough to allow you to ride your bike. After battling to hang on to your bike for the one-and-three-quarter mile (2.8 km) descent, at the bottom of Stonethwaite Fell, the path is firm enough to ride.

The last mile-and-half (2.4 km) of the ride to Rosthwaite contains some of the sweetest cycling moments you are likely to enjoy. Particularly if you have timed your journey to get you to the Riverside Arms during opening hours.

Facilities

AMBLESIDE
A busy town at the heart of the Lake District's busiest area: during the season, the traffic jams can back up towards Windermere. There is a large choice of shops, including outdoor equipment and camping places.
Pubs
Golden Rule, Smithy Brow, Ambleside.
Sportsman.
White Lion.
Eating places
Harvest, Compston Road. Tel. (05394) 33151: vegetarian restaurant.
Zeffirelli's, Compston Road. Tel. (05394) 33845: café and pizzeria.
Bikes
Ambleside Mountain Bikes hires from Scotts Café, Waterhead, Ambleside: Tel. (05394) 32014 or 33592.
Lakeland Mountain Bikes, Elterwater, Great Langdale, Nr Ambleside. Book from shop in Staveley: Tel. (0539) 821 748.
Tourist Information Centre
The Old Courthouse, Church Street, Ambleside, Tel. (05394) 32582.

CHAPEL STILE
Village with a post office, a Co-op and a good pub.
Pub
Wainwrights Inn, Chapel Stile: Tel. (09667) 302.

ELTERWATER
A charming, un-touristy Lakeland village with a good pub looking on to a village green tailor-made for Morris dancers.
Pub
Britannia, Elterwater: Tel. (09667) 210.

GRASMERE
Thanks to the Wordsworth connection, one of the busiest villages in the Lake District. There is a good selection of shops, pubs and eating places.
Eating places
Lancrigg Vegetarian Country House Hotel Easedale. Tel. (09665) 317; vegetarian meals.
Pubs
Swan, Grasmere. Tel. (09665) 551.
Wordsworth, Grasmere. Tel. (09665) 592.
Tourist Information Centre
Red Bank Road, Grasmere. Tel. (09665) 245.

LANGDALE
Pubs
New Dungeon Ghyll, Langdale. Tel. (09667) 213.
Old Dungeon Ghyll, Langdale. Tel. (09667) 272.

LITTLE LANGDALE
Small village at the end of Wrynose Pass with a good pub.
Pubs
Three Shires Inn, Little Langdale. Tel. (09667) 215.

chapter 7

LITTLE LANGDALE
to
WINDERMERE LAKE

Towns and villages: Coniston, Hawkshead, Near
Sawrey, Far Sawrey
Lakes: Coniston Water, Esthwaite Water

Introduction to the area

The final leg of the journey brings us back to the popular heart
of the Lake District with some of its best known names and
sights. The descent to the handsome expanse of Coniston Water
marks an end to "rough stuff" mountain biking.

The precipitous rocky tracks of previous sections here give way
to faster travel on minor roads and well-made forest tracks.
Grizedale Forest itself is a maze of tracks – some large forest
roads, others tiny unmade trails – but all of them provide happy
biking for those who prefer to ride their bikes rather than lugging
them on their shoulders.

After negotiating the labyrinth of Grizedale Forest (no easy
task, since the paths are largely unmarked and the map seems
to be of no real help), there is a fast run on metalled road through
the villages of Near and Far Sawrey down to the Windermere
ferry.

Short diversions from the main route can take you to the town
of Coniston, busy in the season with tourists. Also nearby is the
handsome small town of Hawkshead, which has managed to
retain its attractive character despite an annual flood of visitors.

The route

From Little Langdale to Windermere: 11.5 miles (18.4 km).

From Little Langdale to head of Coniston Water, mostly level ride of 4 miles (6.4 km).

From head of Coniston Water to Grizedale Visitor Centre: ascent of 218 yds over 2 miles (200 m over 3.2 km), descent of 175 yds over 0.75 miles (160 m, over 1.2 km).

From Grizedale Visitor Centre to Esthwaite Water: ascent of 150 yds over one mile (138 m over 1.6 km); descent of 175 yds over 0.5 miles (160 m over 0.8 km).

From Esthwaite Water to Windermere ferry, mostly level ride on metalled road for 3.75 miles (5.2 km).

Grade 2.

In the village of Little Langdale look for a narrow lane on the right travelling south and marked "Unsuitable for cars". The lane drops down to ford the River Brathay and then climbs as a rough track into Moss Rigg Wood. Keep to the main path through the wood and you will emerge at High Tilberthwaite Farm.

Pass through the farmyard and pick up a metalled lane which runs down to the A593. Turn right onto this road and then first left on a bridleway (signposted) at Low Yewdale Farm. The track runs across to Boon Crag Farm where it meets the B5285. Turn right, and then left onto a lane signposted "East of Lake", which skirts Coniston Water and takes you towards Grizedale Forest.

Shortly after the entrance for How Head, take the first turning on the left up an unsigned track. Just beyond the five-bar gate is a sign that points the way to Grizedale.

At first, the path is steep, rocky and unrideable. After a quarter of a mile (0.4 km), the track firms up and levels off towards the forest. As you enter the forest, the path climbs again. Half a mile (0.8 km) after entering the forest, you join a wider forest road: continue to the right.

Half a mile (0.8 km) further on, at a fork in the road, take the left turning – and 200 yards (183 m) down this road, take a smaller track to the left which leads down the hill. This provides a good, fast, rough ride for half a mile (0.8 km) down to one of the main cycle tracks that run through the Grizedale Forest. When you reach the track, turn right and follow the road for half a mile (0.8 km) until you reach the Grizedale Forest Visitor Centre.

Immediately opposite the entrance to the Visitor Centre is a path marked "The Silurian Way", which after a short rocky patch leads on to a wide, firm forest road. Even with the help of the Grizedale Forest Guide Map (price 60p from the Visitor Centre) and the Ordnance Survey map, navigating the maze of forest roads can be a bit of a hit-or-miss business since, surprisingly, there are no clear signposts.

At the end of the path up from the Visitor Centre, turn left and continue straight on for half a mile (0.8 km) until you reach a T-junction, where you turn left; after a mile (1.6 km) you come to a metalled road. Turn left and travel down the hill for 200 yards (183 m) until you reach a junction: turn right and ride round the bottom of Esthwaite Water towards Sawrey, eventually joining the B5285 road. En route to the Windermere ferry, you pass the Beatrix Potter house at Hill Top and travel through the neighbouring village of Far Sawrey.

The ferry across Lake Windermere to Bowness normally operates every 20 minutes: the fare for a cyclist and bicycle is 20p.

What you will see

After the rugged, mountain country of the previous sections, from Little Langdale the scenery begins to take on a more mellow but no less beautiful shape. The huge peaks of Scafell and Helvellyn may no longer dominate the view, but there are still some large fells. The Old Man of Coniston, which rises to 2,631 ft (802 m), is frequently wreathed in mist and offers a spectacular backdrop to Coniston Water, which sits at the Old Man's feet.

Grizedale Forest is one of the most fascinating places in the Lake District, with the attraction of being easily accessible to the mountain biker with a number of laid-out cycle tracks (see map). As well as the natural attractions of the wood's flora and fauna (these include red deer, red squirrel, polecat and a wealth

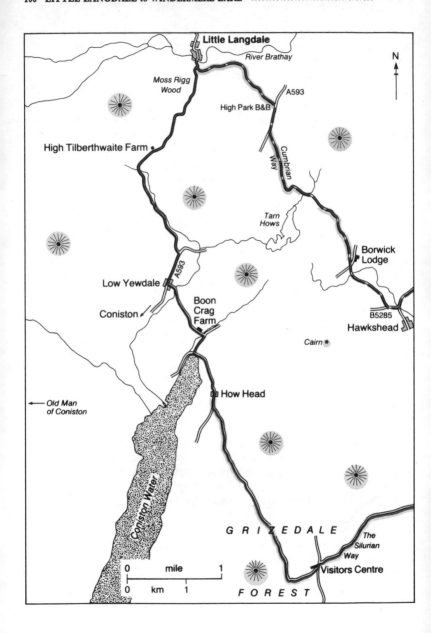

N

Little Langdale

River Brathay

Moss Rigg Wood

A593

High Park B&B

High Tilberthwaite Farm

Cumbrian Way

Tarn Hows

Borwick Lodge

A593

Low Yewdale

Coniston

Boon Crag Farm

B5285

Hawkshead

Cairn

← *Old Man of Coniston*

How Head

G R I Z E D A L E

The Silurian Way

Coniston Water

0 ――― mile ――― 1

0 ――― km ――― 1

Visitors Centre

F O R E S T

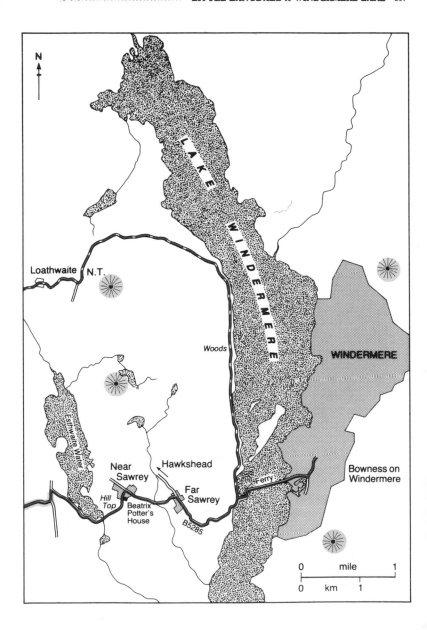

of birds), Grizedale also has the excellent Theatre in the Forest which offers a variety of entertainments.

Near to the Visitor Centre is the site of Grizedale Hall. There were two halls, the first built by Montague Ainslie in 1836; Mr Ainslie planted 1,250,000 larch trees here to provide timbers for his iron mines. A second hall was built in 1903 by Harold Brocklebank, a Liverpool shipping magnate.

The estate was acquired by the Forestry Commission in 1937. During the Second World War it was used as a prisoner-of-war camp for German officers. There was only one successful escaper: Franz von Werra, a Luftwaffe officer, who got away from Grizedale, was recaptured and sent to Canada. From Canada he managed to get to America and then home to Germany: unhappily, after all his efforts he died during the fighting on the Russian front. His story was told in the film *The One Who Got Away*. *The Cage of Eagles*, a recent book by Jim Follett, is a book with its story set in Grizedale POW camp during the war.

The final part of the journey leads along the shore of small, charming Esthwaite Water, passing the Beatrix Potter house at Hill Top Farm before finally reaching journey's end at the ferry stage on Lake Windermere.

Famous connections

The most visited literary residence in the Lake District is not, as you might expect, Wordsworth's Dove Cottage but the former house of Beatrix Potter, Hill Top Farm in Near Sawrey.

Beatrix Potter bought the farm in 1905 three years after the publication of her first book *The Tales of Peter Rabbit*, which astonished the publishing world by selling 50,000 copies in just two years. With the money she earned from *Peter Rabbit* – and two later books, *The Tale of Squirrel Nutkin* and *The Tailor of Gloucester* – she acquired Hill Top.

Hill Top, and the surrounding countryside, were featured in a number of her books, particularly *The Tale of Tom Kitten*, *The Tale of Jemima Puddle-Duck* and *The Tale of Samuel Whiskers*. But although she spent a lot of time at the cottage, and did much of her work there, Hill Top was never her home.

In 1913 she married William Heelis, her solicitor from Hawkshead: they made their home at nearby Castle Cottage. After her marriage she more or less gave up her writing and concentrated on farming, particularly on tending her herds of local Herdwick sheep. She eventually acquired 15 Lake District farms, a total of 4,000 acres of land, which on her death in 1943 at the age of 77 passed into the hands of the National Trust, of which she had been a lifelong supporter.

Her husband's old office in Hawkshead, which also passed to the National Trust, is now the Beatrix Potter Gallery, displaying many of the original water-colours for her books.

Another of Britain's best-loved children's stories, *Swallows and Amazons*, is closely associated with this part of the Lake District. Arthur Mitchell Ransome was born in Leeds in 1884, the eldest of four children. Every year, the family spent the summer holidays in High Nibthwaite, at Swainson's Farm at the southern end of Coniston Water.

Nursing his ambitions of being a writer, in 1913 Ransome went to Russia and found himself in the beginnings of the Russian Revolution. When the First World War started, unfit to join the Army because of poor eye-sight and ill health, he stayed in Russia as a foreign correspondent. He saw the historic events of the Revolution at first hand, knew and talked with Lenin, Trotsky and the other leaders – played chess with Lenin and beat him.

He continued his work as a journalist until 1929. He was asked by the *Manchester Guardian* to go to Berlin as its correspondent. Still troubled by his ill health – piles and an ulcer – he decided to abandon journalism and to concentrate on writing the children's story that he had been considering for several years.

For a tour of *Swallows and Amazons* country, Lanehead makes a good start. This was the home of the Collingwood family who were great friends of Ransome and introduced him to the pleasures of sailing on Coniston Water. Lanehead is probably the model for Beckfoot, the home of the "Amazons": it is now, appropriately enough perhaps, an outdoor pursuits centre.

Next door is the model for Holly Howe, the home of the "Swallows". Bank Ground Farm was the holiday home of the Altounyan family whose children provided the model for the

"Swallows". The house is now a "traditional Lakeland farm-house", offering bed and breakfast. The house is prominently featured at the beginning of the *Swallows and Amazons* film, when the children arrive at the start of their holiday.

Arthur Ransome died on 3 June 1967 at Cheadle Royal Hospital near Manchester. His ashes were buried, according to his wishes, at St Paul's Church, Rusland. The visitors' book in the church shows that Ransome has not been forgotten.

From 1779 to 1787 Wordsworth was a pupil at Archbishop Sandys' Grammar School in Hawkshead. The school is now a museum which preserves what is claimed to be Wordsworth's desk (it has the initials "WW" carved into it). The museum also has the housekeeping ledger of Ann Tyson, the lady with whom Wordsworth lodged in a house now called Wordsworth Lodge (not open to the public).

John Ruskin, the art critic, writer and philosopher, lived at Brantwood, on the east shore of Coniston, not far from the "Swallows and Amazons" houses. Brantwood was Ruskin's home from 1872 until his death in 1900: open to the public, it contains a large collection of Ruskin's drawings and water-colours.

It is claimed that Ruskin was one of the greatest figures of the Victorian age: "a social revolutionary who challenged the moral foundations of 19th-century Britain".

A pioneer conservationist, according to the Russian author Tolstoy: "He was one of those rare men who think with their hearts, and so he thought and said not only what he himself had seen and felt, but what everyone will think and say in the future."

Next to the house is a Wainwright Room, dedicated to the work of the author of the seven-volume *Pictorial Guide to the Lakeland Fells*, which has totalled combined sales of over one million. The room contains Wainwright's desk, pipe, a pair of boots and first editions of his books and original drawings.

Perhaps Coniston's most famous modern connection is with the Campbell family and their attempts on the water speed record on Coniston Water. Sir Malcolm Campbell first came to Coniston in 1939 and established a new record of 141 m.p.h.

After the death of his father, Donald Campbell took up the

challenge with the tireless assistance of Sir Malcolm's mechanic Leo Villa. Donald set his first world record on Ullswater of 202 m.p.h. – but he later set another record on Coniston. On 4 January 1967 Donald Campbell was at Coniston with *Bluebird* to make one more effort – this time to break the 300 m.p.h. barrier. On his final pass, during which he exceeded 300 m.p.h., *Bluebird* somersaulted and smashed apart: Donald Campbell's body was never recovered. Both Campbell and his mechanic Leo Villa are honoured with a memorial in the town centre.

Other routes in the area

Turning the route into a circuit.
20.5 miles (32.8 km).
Journey as above to Windermere ferry.
From Windermere ferry to Borwick Lodge, near Tarn Hows, mostly level ride of 6.25 miles (10 km).
From Borwick Lodge to top of Tarn Hows climb of 109 yds over 1.25 miles (100 m over 2 km).
Descent from top of Tarn Hows to Little Langdale 152 yds over 2.5 miles (139 m over 4 km).
9.5 miles (15.2 km) on metalled roads.
Grade 2.

Follow the main route as outlined above. When you reach the sign warning of the "8T weight limit on ferry" and "No coaches or HGV's . . . on ferry 350 yards ahead", take the unsigned road which runs to the left of this sign.

This is a good, firm forest road that follows the shore of Lake Windermere in its early stages before climbing a little way up into the woods. After two-and-a-half miles (4 km) you reach a main road: turn left in the direction of Hawkshead.

Before turning to the right, after one-and-a-quarter miles (2 km) at the National Trust sign for Loathwaite, look out on the left for the ornamental horse-trough marked with the date 1891 and the touching note "In memory of happy days".

On reaching the B5286 turn left, and then immediately right on the B5285 towards Coniston. One hundred yards (91 m) up this road, immediately after the saw mills, turn right again.

After half a mile (0.8 km) turn towards Ambleside: 100 yards (91 m) further on, opposite the entrance to Borwick House, go up the path marked "Unsuitable for motor cars". This is the Cumbrian Way which climbs up towards Tarn Hows. The path is mostly rideable – but there are a number of dangerous patches of loose stones, particularly on the steeper parts.

The Cumbrian Way eventually meets the A593: turn right towards Ambleside: 400 yards (366 m) on the left take the turning marked "High Park B&B". Follow the road until the ford which leads across to Little Langdale.

Circuit from Coniston via the Walna Scar Road: 11.5 miles (18.5 km).

Ascent of 590 yds over 3.4 miles (540 m over 5.5 km) from Coniston to summit beside Brown Pike.

Descent of 142 yds over 0.8 miles (130 m over 1.3 km) from summit to old mine workings.

Descent 197 yds over 2 miles (180 m over 3.6 km) from Dawson Pike to Stephenson Ground.

5 miles (8 km) on metalled roads.

Grade 3.

From Coniston take the narrow lane signposted "Sun Hotel". Pass the hotel, bear right at the junction and follow the tarmacked road to the car park. From here footpaths go right to Coniston Old Man and left to Bleathwaite. Take the good track straight ahead. Apart from a few awkward rocky sections the track is good until close to the summit of the Walna Scar Road's course alongside Brown Pike.

Pass a large cairn, then cross Cove Bridge. As you approach the summit there is a neat stone shelter to the right of the path.

The descent is good, cutting a clean diagonal down the fell. Where the path turns sharply downhill towards a gate turn sharp left, before the gate. Here you leave the Walna Scar Road and pass through old quarry workings. Once past the workings the way becomes boggy in places but still clear on the ground as it picks a way through crags and begins to descend alongside the River Lickle. Keep to the right of the stream and the path, vague at first, becomes more distinct as it nears Stephenson Ground.

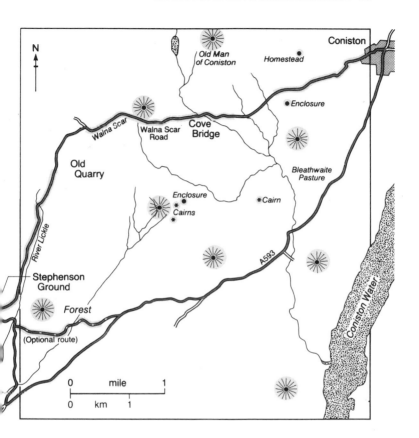

When you meet a lane, turn left. Once over a stream you will see a bridleway sign pointing into the woods to the left. You have a choice of route here. You can either go through the woods, a tough and somewhat frustrating ride which you may not feel is worth the effort, or follow lanes back to Coniston.

First the forest route.

Take the well-waymarked path up through the trees, climbing steeply and crossing two forestry tracks. At the third forestry track go left, then first right on another broad track and across a stream. After 50 yards turn right up a narrow path. At the summit you meet another forestry track. Go straight across.

From here the trees have been recently felled and the waymarking ends. Follow the very rough track as it runs along the hillside parallel to a track down in the valley to the right. After a few hundred yards the path swings right and descends to this track. Turn left and cycle up to a gate which leads out of the forest onto a lane. Turn left and follow the lane down to the A593.

To avoid the forestry section, follow the lane past the woods until a fork. Go left and follow the lane down to the A593.

Linking route from Coniston to the Hardknott Pass for Boot and Eskdale: 8 miles (12.8 km).

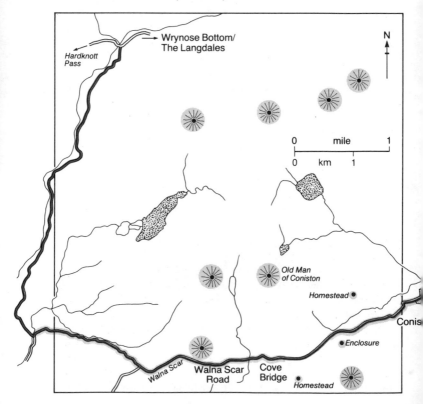

Ascent of 590 yds over 3.4 miles (540 m over 5.5 km) from
Coniston to summit beside Brown Pike.
Descent of 492 yds over 1.6 miles (450 m over 2.6 km).
3 miles (4.8 km) on metalled roads.
Grade 3.

From Coniston take the narrow lane signposted "Sun Hotel".
Pass the hotel, bear right at the junction and follow the
tarmacked road to the car park. From here footpaths go right to
Coniston Old Man and left to Bleathwaite. Take the good track
straight ahead. Apart from a few awkward rocky sections the
track is good until close to the summit of Walna Scar.

Pass a large cairn, then cross Cove Bridge. As you approach
the summit there is a neat stone shelter to the right of the path.

The descent is good, cutting a clean diagonal down the fell.
Where the path turns sharply downhill, follow it through a gate
and over a very rough, rocky and exhilarating section and down
to a lane. Go left, continue straight on at a T-junction and right
at the next junction, where a sign points to "The Langdales via
Wrynose".

Follow the lane for three miles (4.8 km) until a junction. Turn
left to go over Hardknott Pass, right to the Langdales.

Linking route from Seathwaite to Eskdale: 4 miles (6.4 km).
From Seathwaite to Kepple Crag climb of 273 yds over 2.75
miles (250 m over 4.4 km).
From Kepple Crag to Eskdale, descent of 347 yds over 1.25 miles
(317 m over 2 km).
No metalled roads.
Grade 4.

Take an unsigned path that begins between the two buildings
opposite the Newfield Inn. Follow this level track across the
bridges and through a series of gates until you reach a
farmhouse: from here the path to Grassguard is signposted.

The early section is steep and stony, but as you approach the
top of the slope the path levels off and takes you to the right
along the top of the slope. After a further series of gates, passing
through a farmhouse right beside the kitchen window, almost,

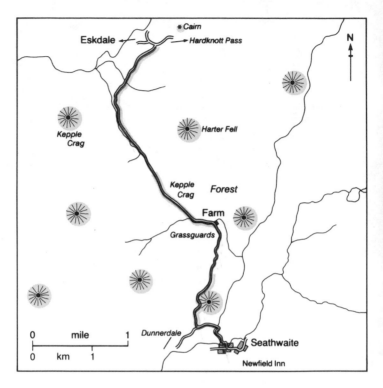

the path climbs up beyond Grassguard through the forest towards Kepple Crag.

The road up through the forest is steep but well made – quite rideable if you have the stamina. As you approach the final section of the forest, in the shadow of Harter Fell, the way becomes very rocky: you will need to carry your bike for almost all the rest of the way.

On leaving the forest, the landscape below Harter Fell is bleak and slightly ominous – particularly if a mist is gathering on the high peaks. Keep to the fence, which will lead you towards Hardknott Pass.

After a few yards, you reach a stile. On crossing the stile, and the small stream, follow the steep path down the valley side to the road at the bottom.

Facilities

CONISTON
A cheerful lakeside town with a good range of hotels, shops, pubs and eating-places.
Pubs
Crown Hotel, Coniston LA21 8EA. Tel. (053 94) 41243.
Ship Inn, Coniston. Tel. (053 94) 41224.
Bank Ground Farm, Coniston, Cumbria. Tel. (053 94) 41264: the model for Holly Howe in Ransome's *Swallows and Amazons*. Offers bed-and-breakfast accommodation.
Bikes
Summitreks, 14 Yewdale Road, Coniston, Cumbria LA21 8DU. Tel. (053 94) 41212.
Tourist Information Centre
16 Yewdale Road, Coniston. Tel. (053 94) 41533.

HAWKSHEAD
Very picturesque small Lakeland town – too picturesque for some tastes perhaps – but charming nevertheless. Good range of shops, pubs and eating-places.
Pubs
The Drunken Duck, Barngates, Nr Hawkshead. Tel. (096 66) 347.
King's Arms, The Square, Hawkshead. Tel. (096 66) 372.
Queen's Arms, Hawkshead. Tel. (096 66) 271.
Tourist information Centre
Main Car Park, Hawkshead. Tel. (096 66) 525.

SAWREY
Divided into two villages: Near Sawrey and Far Sawrey. Near Sawrey is famous as the home of Beatrix Potter. Near Sawrey is near Grizedale Forest, which has an excellent Visitor Centre: Tel. (0229) 860272.
Pubs
Sawrey Hotel, Far Sawrey. Tel. (096 62) 3425.
Tower Bank Arms, Near Sawrey. Tel. (096 66) 334: owned by the National Trust.
Bikes
Grizedale Mountain Bikes, Old Hall Car Park, Grizedale Forest Centre. Tel. (0229) 860369.